OFF-ROAD RACING

Other Lyle Kenyon Engel books:

OFF-ROAD RACING

Produced by Lyle Kenyon Engel

Text by Monty Norris
Edited by George Engel and Marla Ray

DODD, MEAD & COMPANY · NEW YORK

ISBN: 0–396–06867–7
Library of Congress Catalog Card Number: 73–11553
Printed in the United States of America

CONTENTS

INTRODUCTION

When I was assigned to cover my first off-road race in Baja California I was barely aware of what the event was all about. I wasn't alone. I soon found out that my ignorance was shared by a large number of drivers entered in the grueling and rugged event. Perhaps that realization gave me my first major insight into the nature, even the essence, of this unusual sport. For off-road racing is different from its older and more sophisticated cousins such as sports car and oval track racing.

Why is it different? Because in most forms of motor competition winning is *everything*, it is the single major goal of any race driver worthy of putting a helmet on and fastening his seat belt. It is certainly an honorable goal, one that serves as an outlet for man's incurable instinct to compete—either against himself or others—to achieve some degree and variety of perfection. And auto racing, perhaps more that any other human test of skill, demands perfection. Continuous perfection while usually enduring mental and physical discomfort. But in off-road racing, at least for many of its devotees, the challenge is different. The off-road racer is really out there to challenge himself and experience the unknown. To try the impossible and once in a while succeed. It's a way of leaving all the neat, clearly defined patterns of behavior at home for a confrontation with chaos.

If a road racer breaks his equipment he coasts to the side and sadly walks back to the pits where, in a matter of minutes, he may relax with a beer and grumble to his friends about his rotten luck. But if an off-road racer breaks down he may spend hours in the scorching sun or freezing night just waiting for a lift to the nearest checkpoint where he may have to curl up in the back of a truck and wait another day or two before returning home.

That kind of challenge demands a much different psychology. For the off-road racer survival and finishing the course are as important as winning. The motorcyclist or dune buggy driver who can say he completed a race is a winner in the minds of most of his peers and certainly the followers. Whether he was first in his class or last, he is a walking, breathing success story—a hero. And after watching dozens of backbreaking, machine-busting derbies I would never question the validity and worth of such worship.

But as a born skeptic who had covered motor racing in all its crazy forms from Nürburgring to Riverside, I was something less than admiring or enthusiastic about the idea of Mr. and Mrs. Middle America playing Juan Fangio on the dusty roads and trails of Baja California. To put it frankly, I thought they were crazy. I had traveled much of the peninsula myself, and I couldn't think of many places in that primitive land where a vehicle could travel safely at more than 15 or 20 miles an hour—in *daylight*! And these, whatever you could find to call them, would be tackling much of the terrain in the black of night. There are few places on this globe where it gets darker when the sun goes down than Baja California! What's more, in most forms of motor racing, competitors learn every detail of the course usually before they even attempt to qualify for a starting position. They know within a fraction of a second when to tap the brakes, when to shift. But that would be impossible in Baja, I thought, for a number of reasons. First, most of the entrants would not have the time to pre-run the course. Secondly, with weather conditions such as they are in that part of the world a pre-run would be almost useless. Smooth stretches of dry lake could turn into rivers or swamps overnight after a heavy rainstorm. Narrow, treacherous trails along some ridge might disappear down the mountainside.

Civilization has not made much of an impression on Baja California, or many of its residents. Few areas in the northern hemisphere are more hostile to human survival. That's why the idea of using the semitropical peninsula as a playground for motor vehicles seemed nothing short of absurd to me. Sure, there would no doubt be a few hardy and lucky souls who would complete the miserable 832-mile trek from the seaside city of Ensenada to La Paz near the tip of Baja. But how long would civilized, rational, comfort-loving Americans continue to endure such unnecessary nonsense? Not for long, I was convinced. But I completely misjudged my fellow man and woman, and their instinct for survival and sense of adventure. For not only do they return to Baja twice a year to compete, but new races are being added to the calendar all the time.

As with most sports in their infancy, off-road racing is done more for love than money, although a handful of drivers are able to make a living at it through the aid of sponsor money and skillful bookkeeping. One such modern hero and off-road super star is soft-spoken Johnny Johnson of Spring Valley, a former Volkswagen mechanic who got the dune buggy fever early and garnered his mechanical genius and driving skill into a lucrative career. Car builders and motorcycle riders are finding it less difficult each year to interest sponsors in sharing expenses, but for every high budget effort entered in an off-road race there will still be thirty others built with undying enthusiasm and spare parts in somebody's garage by friends and neighbors.

The first major race was held in Baja California in November 1967, and attracted little attention from general news media. Most of us in the business considered the race little more than another crazy circus staged by a handful of car and motorcycle nuts—the kind of thing that happens regularly in fad-crazy Southern California. That first race started in Tijuana, just across the border from San Diego, where entrants rallied to Ensenada before embarking on the rough, high-speed trip south to La Paz. To say we underestimated the widespread interest in the event, and the growing popularity of off-road events in general, is a classic understatement. Within hours after the cars began leaving Ensenada, a small seaport town about 65 miles below the border, calls began pouring in to the newsroom from throughout the entire country (as far east as New Jersey) from folks wanting to know how Uncle Harry, Cousin Charlie or George-Down-the-Street were doing in the race. (Even one of our switchboard operators, who had complained earlier about the number of callers, finally broke down and asked if we had any idea how her neighbor, so-and-so, was doing.) Zap! A new sport was born!

Since that first race, of course, off-road racing has spawned an entirely new industry to collect consumer dollars and at the same time feed the pockets of promoters and some drivers. The total purse at most off-road events in those first years would be barely enough to put new tires on the winner's car. Today prize money and accessory cash from various manufacturers has pushed the total cash offering at some events to more than $100,000—and it grows each year. Business has been quick to capitalize on what it recognized immediately as a wide-open marketplace. The new products now available to the off-road racing enthusiast are countless. Several manufacturers are coming out with special "Baja Proven" tires, wheels, batteries, gloves, seats, helmets, shock absorbers, roll bars, *ad infinitum.*

But while big business has invaded off-road racing, the sport still belongs to the same people who created it—mechanics, housewives, doctors, secretaries, engineers, school teachers, milkmen—the guy next door. Tracing the origins of the sport can be as difficult as finishing one of the many spine-shattering races. Some off-road veterans insist the genealogy of the sport dates back to the 1920s when speed freaks rigged their Model T Fords with caterpillar-type belts for better traction and took off across brush-covered fields after jack rabbits. The glut of surplus four-wheel-drive vehicles available after World II added to the growing interest in "outback" off-road driving. But it remained for Bruce Meyers, an imaginative boatbuilder from Newport Beach, California, to really get things rolling in the early 1960s when he took a wrecked Volkswagen and stripped it down to frame, suspension, engine and running gear, then slapped on a fiberglass body and called it—what else?—a *dune buggy*. The Meyers Manx, as he dubbed it, quickly became one of the hottest-selling items on four wheels in car-crazy Southern California. But not even Meyers, an affable, rugged-looking outdoorsman, had the remotest idea of what his inexpensive little creation would someday inspire.

Monty Norris
San Diego, California

Mike Patrick crosses the finish line after 10 hours 8 minutes of grueling desert racing in the 1969 Mint 400. He shared victory with Phil Bowers, and the team returned the next year for a repeat performance. More than 100 motorcycles usually enter the annual race held each March in the Nevada desert near Las Vegas.

1 HEADING FOR THE BOONDOCKS

———————————————————————→

Felix Mendoza, his round face tanned and weathered from hard years in the cruel desert sun, smiled proudly as he showed a visitor the battered remains of an aging dune buggy. The rusting hulk waited forlornly in the blistering midday sun, covered with fine white Baja California dust. Mendoza, who looks much older than his fifty-two years, talked enthusiastically about his plans for the old racer as he sipped warm bottled beer. All four of the buggy's rotted tires were flat. The Volkswagen engine mounted in the rear listed severely to one side, nearly touching the ground.

"It was left here two years ago," he said in Spanish. "Two men pushed it in here one night very late. They used the bathroom, then bought all the beer I had and walked on into town. I never saw them again.

1

"It needs a lot of work, but I figure that with all the cars that are left around here each year it won't be long before I can get it running just like new."

Felix Mendoza operates a gas station on the northern outskirts of El Rosario, Baja California, some 150 miles south of the U.S./ Mexico border. Each November dune buggies, sedans, four-wheel-drive vehicles and motorcycles roar past his station as they head south another seven hundred miles to La Paz and the finish of the famed Mexican 1000 off-road race. Many of them limp slowly past his station, however. And some, like the pitiful dune buggy sitting around in back, don't travel any farther.

What does Felix plan to do with the dune buggy if and when he gets it running?

"Just race around in the hills and chase jack rabbits," he answered.

How about entering the race, Felix? After all, you know this part of the country like few others. Felix smiles and shakes his head no. "That's crazy," he says. "Too dangerous."

Maybe he's right, but some four hundred adventure-thirsty *gringos* come to Baja California twice a year to compete in wild, bone-busting off-road races—which are really held on roads of sorts. Of course the Mexican definition of a road would not be found in an American dictionary, but they *are* used as roads every day by local citizenry. True a lot of cattle, horses and goats share these dusty and rutted byways, but . . .

Describing off-road racing to the uninitiated is itself a challenge to the English language. Partly, at least, because the best descriptive words come in four letters and upset little old ladies and most church folk. It's a sport that demands more stamina than skill, although without lots of each anyone seriously considering a try at the game would be much better off wrestling a gorilla. He'd probably have a better chance of getting away unbruised.

After completing his first off-road event in the Baja 500 a couple of years ago, Indianapolis veteran Walley Dallenbach declined to sit down, and eagerly grabbed some liquid refreshment instead, as he weakly proclaimed, "That's the longest —— 500 miles I've ever traveled in my life!"

Maybe just to see if it's really like that all the time, Dallenbach came back again the next year . . . and the next . . .

"It's just so damned much fun," he said one morning before a race. "Crazy, yes. But a helluva lot of fun." His face and white driving suit were clean then. So were those of his rotund partner, Jack Allison. That would change soon. Within about another ninety minutes both would resemble a couple of cowpokes who'd been on the trail six months. It was still an hour before they were scheduled to be flagged off the line in Ensenada, one minute behind the guy ahead of them, and one minute ahead of the guy behind them. That's the way it's usually done in off-road events. It makes things safer, but more important, it gives everyone an equal opportunity since the real adversary in this kind of racing is *time*.

Although there is some heavy wheel-to-wheel dueling occasionally, the object in off-road events is to get from Point A to Point B in the shortest amount of time. Now suppose, for example, that you leave Point A at noon and arrive at the finish (Point B) at four o'clock in the afternoon. Meanwhile, farther down the entry list, I have to wait until half past twelve to start on my way, and don't arrive at Point B until quarter past four or fifteen minutes after you arrived. You've already had a beer while waiting for me, but I still win because I completed the distance in three hours and forty-five minutes compared with your run of four hours flat.

Of course when actually computing the times of some three hundred entries leaving at one-minute intervals over a period of, say, five hours—and traveling five hundred to perhaps nearly a thousand miles—it gets tricky and difficult to compute. Problems do arise, and drivers often argue bitterly (but rarely successfully) about their times. One year a motorcycle rider in the Mexican 1000 roared into La Paz nearly an hour ahead of the next arrival. But the second finisher, in a dune buggy, proved to be the overall winner of that grueling event. He had left nearly *two hours* after the motorcycle team, which changed riders in El Arco at the halfway point, and therefore toured the distance in nearly a full hour less time.

Wheel-to-wheel racing, mentioned earlier, is generally discouraged in off-road racing both for sporting reasons and safety. Rules usually require slower cars or motorcycles to let faster vehicles pass. But, of course, out in the desert anything can happen—and now and then some guy will play games with another competitor. But those stunts, most drivers agree, are rare and the clowns who perform them are often wise not to come back again. (Off-road enthusiasts are generally a rugged lot, and they have effective ways of handling such problems privately.) Besides, there are more than enough challenges in most such events—dodging ruts, trying to see through all the dust and keeping the car or bike rightside up—without resorting to a game of Russian roulette with another driver or rider. After all, an off-road course is not Daytona Speedway, and in most places there is little or no room for two vehicles to ride along side-by-side, let alone play high-speed footsie!

What Do They Drive?

More off-road cars were born in junkyards than probably any other variety of racing machine in the world. But don't let that fool

Off-road racers spend nearly as much time in the air as on the rough ground, as this buggy pilot demonstrates as he charges out of a wash in the Mint 400.

you. The sport also has its super-sophisticated, mind-boggling, hairy-sounding, fire-breathing monsters that carry a price tag large enough to make even John Paul Getty raise an eyebrow . . . momentarily. But such exotic rigs still remain in the minority at almost any meet, from Searchlight, Nevada, to Ensenada, Baja California.

Sure, you say. The fancy rigs may be in a minority, but it's that well-financed elite who take home all the ribbons and trophies and money and whatever. Well, that comforting, defeatist attitude may work for some people, but it doesn't have a place in off-road racing.

"The thing to remember is that just going the fastest isn't always good enough," says veteran off-road racer and Baja champion Andy DeVercelly Jr. "You have to get everything working—speed, equipment, driving. Sure big money helps, but that's *all* it does—help. It won't work magic!"

Off-road racing is open to a variety of motor vehicles from 50cc motorcycles to V8-powered Ford Broncos. In between lies a colorful array of equipment limited in scope only by human imagination and ingenuity. As they say in the carnival business, "Something for everyone!" (Got an old taxi, you say? Step right up, my boy, and I can show you how to turn that old critter into a slick Baja Buggy in . . .)

Doug Fortin and Dick Clark began their success story in a junkyard. They had a dream, but not much money. "I didn't have money to buy a buggy, and without any experience or a big name, I knew I wasn't going to get a ride in somebody else's car," Fortin explained.

His logic seemed fairly solid. But Doug Fortin wasn't about to give up. That's just not his style. Fortin sat down with his friend Dick Clark and they sipped a few beers and worked out a plan. First stop was a junkyard where Fortin bought a tired six-cylinder, air-cooled Corvair engine. As he saved up the money, he would buy Army surplus Jeep parts. Every night and on weekends the duo worked long hours rebuilding the engine and designing their racer.

Slowly the pile of rusty and greasy springs, shocks, nuts, bolts, tubes and other gadgets that had been stacked here and there were assembled into a sleek two-seater dune buggy with a rear-mounted engine and four-wheel drive. It wasn't the kind of rig that catches the eye of camera buffs wandering through pits before a race—you know, the guys who ogle chrome-plated, candy-colored things that make terrifying sounds. No, it was nothing like that. In fact it was pretty damned ugly. It was sort of a yellow color with a big roll cage over the seats and big headlamps mounted on top above the driver's head. Not really much to look at, but then eight hundred dollars doesn't buy much of a race car these days. Or does it?

Maybe not if you're looking for beauty. But beauty and off-road racing don't seem to mix. The same year that Fortin and Clark put together their homemade rig they scored a class victory in the rugged Baja 500 that starts and ends in Ensenada after a bouncy, dusty swing through some of the western hemisphere's toughest terrain. The team also has won major events in Las Vegas at the prestigious Mint 400 Desert Rally and at the Riverside Grand Prix for dune buggies. Another rags-to-riches success story? Not at all. Fortin and Clark are probably more typical of the off-road racer than someone like legendary Parnelli Jones, the oval track hero who steps into a $35,000 specially-made Ford Bronco and roars off into the desert with a "win or bust" philosophy.

"I guess this car is worth about a million bucks in sweat and labor and busted knuckles," Fortin mused one afternoon in his garage. "I think Dick and I have proved you can still race on a small budget—at least in off-road racing.

"We started dead last (in the Baja 500), and frankly neither of us thought we had a chance in hell of winning. We weren't too confident of even finishing!"

The popularity of off-road racing has even spread to the college classroom. For a group of seven students from Cal Poly in Pomona, California, the Baja 500 was the final examination for a semester of race car building. The car was a late model Ford sedan, painted bright yellow, pieced together from parts of four used taxis donated to the youths by a Los Angeles cab company. The car was dubbed, naturally, the "Baja Taxi." The project was sponsored by the Cal

6

Poly chapter of the Society of Automotive Engineers.

"Most of the parts were donated to us by various companies," explained Peter Sigwardt, one of the students involved in the project. "If we had had to pay for everything ourselves this car would have cost us over $4000."

But instead, according to Sigwardt, the students put the car in off-road racing condition for about $300.

At the opposite end of the equipment spectrum are the super fast Ford Broncos prepared by racing wizard Bill Stroppe at his shop in Long Beach, California. Stroppe usually builds about half a dozen of these impressive rigs for the major off-road races in Mexico and also the big 400-miler each year in Las Vegas. Parnelli Jones always handles the driving chores of the number-one machine with a daring and silent Stroppe riding shotgun. Powered by a solid 350-cubic-inch Ford V8, the Broncos have no equal when it comes to acceleration or top speed. And the brilliant Parnelli squeezes every ounce of performance out of the machine that Stroppe's genius was able to come up with in the shop.

But it would be silly, of course, to pit a beast like the Bronco against, say, a Volkswagen-powered dune buggy or a Ford sedan. That's where classes or categories come into the picture.

There are several organizations and local clubs staging off-road races throughout the Southwestern United States, and each has its own particular set of rules governing competition and dividing cars and motorcycles into classes. But most of them follow the same general pattern in trying to keep things fair and equitable. Although again it is important to remember that each group may vary its rules concerning competition classes, the most common separations are as follows: Category 1—Production two-wheel-drive passenger vehicles. Category 2—Production two-wheel-drive utility (pickup truck) vehicles. Category 3—Production two-wheel-drive buggies. Category 4—Nonproduction two-wheel-drive vehicles. Category 5 —Production four-wheel-drive vehicles. Category 6—Nonproduction four-wheel-drive buggies. Category 7—Motorcycles of 125cc and under. Category 8—Motorcycles over 125cc. Category 9— VW Baja Bugs.

7

Although the Baja and Las Vegas races always attract a wide variety of machines, many off-road clubs restrict their events to dune buggies. Other clubs confine membership to production four-wheel-drive rigs like the Bronco or Jeep. Motorcycle riders dominated many major off-road events in the early years, but growing technology among car builders, along with a polishing of driving skills, has now almost completely reversed that situation. No motorcycle has scored an overall victory in Baja since the 1968 Mexican 1000, and the two-wheelers compete separately on a different day in the wild and punishing Las Vegas Mint 400.

"We do this for strictly safety reasons," explained Mel Larson, race director of the Mint meet. "Putting bikes on the same course with cars would be unnecessarily dangerous. Most of the bike riders seem to like it better that way, too."

Jeeps and other four-wheel-drive vehicles were among the first machines used in off-roading. Growing popularity of the sport, however, has attracted nearly every kind of two- and four-wheel contraption imaginable, many invented strictly for the burgeoning new sport.

In Baja races motorcyclists get the green flag first, with roughly a thirty-minute interval before the first four-wheeler is waved off. This is done to give the riders a good head start, so that only a few of the very fastest cars will overtake them.

But the dune buggy—a tubular-frame, open-wheel, rear-engine machine—is the pure off-road vehicle in the minds of many fans and drivers. What these little rigs may lack in power and appearance they quickly make up for in handling and that nebulous component—charisma. The origin of their high ranking in the off-road racing world is hidden in the notion that off-road racing belongs, or should belong, to folks who make their own equipment. Or else drive homemade equipment. Often ignored, however, is the fact that a good percentage of dune buggies today are built by a growing but still small corps of manufacturers springing up mostly in the sprawling Los Angeles metropolitan area. (But at least they *look* homemade.)

The VW-powered dune buggy is now considered the norm, a standard upon which to base any variation in design. All other buggies are considered hybrids. What folks soon forget is that the much revered VW buggy is itself a hybrid. (And in Southern California and environs *that* sort of talk is blasphemous!)

Many buffs throughout the Southwest snickered at such creations as the Baja Boot, a four-wheel-drive machine powered by the Chevrolet Camaro 350-cubic-inch V8 engine, and using the Chevy 396 high performance Turbo Hydramatic transmission, Dana transfer case and Corvette rear drive assembly.

The Baja Boot was the brainchild of former General Motors engineer Vic Hickey, a pioneer off-roader who now operates his own research and development firm in Ventura, California, north of Los Angeles. Hickey designed the Boot in his spare time before he parted ways with GM. From drawing board to testing ground, the project took only thirty days. This was made possible by a group of Hickey's colleagues who volunteered their spare time to help out. Always safety conscious, Hickey incorporated many features into his racers to prevent injuries in some of the wild spills that are commonplace in off-road events. To ease the driving chore he used the rugged Saginaw power steering gear with two turns lock to lock, disc brakes all around and a collapsible steering column. The big V8 engine in the Boot is mounted facing backward just ahead of the rear axle shafts in what is known as mid-engine fashion. The powerplant is water-cooled by a large Chevy truck radiator mounted on the extreme rear of the frame, with a special 20-inch-diameter six-blade fan that has reverse pitch to blow air away from the engine and through the radiator.

About a year and a half after the introduction of the first Baja Boot, Hickey produced a smaller version dubbed the Mini Boot, using a Chevy II four-cylinder engine. The cars were brilliantly designed and built, but they never completely caught the fancy of off-roaders. Maybe it was the five-digit price tag that scared some away, but most racers seem to agree that a water-cooled buggy is more trouble than it's usually worth.

"You want to keep things as simple as possible," said Andy DeVercelly. "And adding a radiator is just adding another headache."

Despite the fascination for the little open-wheel buggies, production four-wheel-drive vehicles still capture their share of admirers and followers. Among the more successful members of the production four-wheel-drive clan is Brian Chuchua, a Southern California Jeep dealer with a long and impressive record in off-road competition. Chuchua, who also conducts the prestigious annual Riverside Grand Prix, often enters a team of five or six modified Jeep vehicles in events. And these machines frequently capture as much attention from other drivers and fans as the exotic buggies and Broncos.

One of Chuchua's more creative entries into the off-road world was a four-wheel-drive mid-engine Jeepster powered with a 390-cubic-inch V8 engine. "Off-road races are rarely won on horsepower," Chuchua explained. (Although Parnelli Jones remains unconvinced.) "And the mid-engine car will always handle better because the engine location takes weight off the front axle. That way you're less apt to have front axle damage, too."

Another Chuchua creation that caused quite a stir was his V6-powered, two-wheel-drive racer covered with a fiberglass body. Some skeptics considered the car unsafe and unsound for the bruising it would take in Mexico. But Chuchua disappointed his critics in grand fashion when the car flipped one year in the Mexican 1000 and recovered well enough and quickly enough to still garner a fifth place finish in its class. Chuchua's vehicles have won their class several times in the Baja 500, the Mexican 1000 and the Mint 400 in Las Vegas.

But for every sophisticated, well-endowed operation like that of Bill Stroppe's Bronco-building concern or Vic Hickey's outfit, there exist perhaps two dozen or more small shops producing less than a handful of buggies or some such off-road vehicle each year, usually on an order basis. One such firm is Bonnie's Baby Buggies of Encinitas, California, a small beach community a few miles north of San Diego.

The bulk of work (and income) at Bonnie's, according to owner and operator Pete Springer, is general machining. Springer is co-owner of the business with his father, Fred. It was Pete Springer's interest in off-road racing and driving dune buggies that led to his entry into the manufacture of them.

Sturdy rollbars can be lifesavers in case of a flip. But when the going gets rough, as it usually does, they also provide something to hold on to.

"There is a great distinction between dune buggies and the off-road racers," he said. "And we have turned out both. The racers are built just for that, to race, and they ride very stiff because of the suspension, which has to take rough terrain at high speeds."

Springer not only builds VW buggies from the ground up, but also modifies stock Volkswagens to run in the Baja Bug division of off-road events. Baja Bugs are basically VW Beetles with the front and rear body work bobbed and minor suspension changes to make them tougher and more stable. Details on how to prepare a Baja Bug appear in Chapter 4.

"We also do the machine work for parts for dune buggies," the younger Springer continued. "And we specialize in new ideas and new applications of design and engineering for these vehicles. For example I made one entirely out of aluminum and as far as I know there are not more than five all-aluminum buggies in the world."

Okay, fine. Sounds like a heads-up operation all around. But why the name "Bonnie's Baby Buggies"?

Springer smiles patiently at the question. Bonnie is his wife's name and she also happens to double as office manager at the shop. Springer said he wanted to get her name into the buggy end of the business somehow, and simply picked "Bonnie's Baby Buggies" because it sounded good. "Bonnie's Buggy" didn't quite have the right ring.

"We started with 'Bonnie' and just added 'Baby Buggies' for the whim of it, just for the alliteration," he said.

Springer became interested in dune buggies in the mid-sixties, and eventually gravitated to off-road racing.

"After about three years of racing as a hobby," he said, "I decided one day that I could build those cars, so that's how the idea took hold and how the work started. We have three to six employees, according to the number of jobs in the plant, and while general machine work is our principal volume, the car-making is a new and very interesting part of it. When we build a motor we assemble it entirely from new parts, instead of trying to modify and rebuild the original motor."

Who Runs the Show?

With the sudden popularity of off-road activity, particularly in the Southwest, it stood to reason that the whole business needed to be organized. But racing types, despite what most of them say, have built-in distaste for anything that smacks of organization. They're weekend anarchists, rebels with a cause, a devotion to breaking the pattern of daily trips on the freeways, sitting at a desk in a sterile office, punching a clock, bolting down a bologna sandwich during lunch, yes sir, no sir, right away sir. Phooey!

That's how the dune buggy thing got started. A day in the back-country, just you and the buggy and the breeze smacking you on the chin. (Hey, Charlie! A six-pack says I can git up that hill yonder 'fore you. Okay, ol' buddy, you're on. Hope that beer's plenty cold!) But just roaming the hills and playing games on warm sunny Sunday afternoons doesn't quite make it for most competitive spirits. (Say, Fred. I was out doing my buggy thing yesterday, and, man, you should of seen me wheelin' that little honey around! Oh, really? Gee, that's nice!) Like drag racers on Main Street, U.S.A., bored with stop-light starts and expensive traffic tickets, off-roaders needed a sense of purpose. (Hey, Fred. I finished first in class in the Borrego Rough 100! No kidding! Congratulations, pal. Say, got time for a beer? I wanna hear all about it. First, huh? After all, who's to say a record's a record if no one's keeping score—official like?)

Four-wheel enthusiasts, of course, had the National Four-Wheel-Drive Association and two-wheel followers had the American Motorcycle Association to set standards and stage events. But for a long time dune buggyists had only their enthusiasm, wide-open spaces and Kentucky Fried Chicken. It wasn't enough. The need for something *Or*-ganized kept eating away. People started talking about it. Everyone seemed to agree. *Some kind of group to stage races was needed.* Talk began spreading throughout the Southern California area that something had to be done soon. Why not get a few people together and throw around some ideas? Good idea.

Let's. And someone did. In early 1967 a meeting was called among enthusiasts of various sorts, anyone who might be even remotely interested in forming an association to conduct off-road events. Bigger and better than the sand drags at Pismo Beach or down at Carlsbad.

It was an unlikely gathering: brash motorcycle enthusiasts who preferred rough and tumble back-country riding to slick road racing, eager dune buggy devotees seeking something more challenging than an occasional sprint, hardy four-wheelers wanting some action, veteran motoring journalists anxious to see a new sport born, and nervous auto company representatives vying for a piece of the action.

The outgrowth of that meeting was what eventually became the National Off-Road Racing Association—or NORRA, as it quickly became known. Ed Pearlman, a San Fernando Valley florist and four-wheel-drive buff, was selected president. While incorporation and rule-book writing were still in progress the group began planning its first major event. It was to be a high-speed rally November 1 to 4 from Tijuana, B.C., just across the U.S./Mexico border from San Diego, to La Paz, some 890 miles south near the tip of the primitively beautiful and rugged peninsula. NORRA decided to call it the Mexican 1000. Not perhaps entirely accurate, but it was certainly better than calling it the Baja California 900, or maybe the Peninsula Rally. Pearlman, in much the style of NASCAR founding father Bill France, intended to go at things in a big way. He required a $250 entry fee for each vehicle, and began recruiting sponsor money for cash prizes. Four classes of competition were established for that first event: Category I—production two-wheel-drive vehicles (mass-produced cars and trucks); Category II—production dune buggies; Category III—modified vehicles, such as Broncos and the like, with beefed-up engines; and Category IV—motorcycles. Cash awards of $5000 were posted to top finishers in each class. Not even Pearlman, a strong-willed and self-confident sort, was quite prepared for the eventual success of the race, which quickly attracted international attention. Pearlman capitalized on the success of his first venture, however, and while he was busy

Believe it or not, this is considered pretty good road down Baja California way, and speed king Mickey Thompson uses this kind of relatively smooth terrain to make up time in his powerful Chevrolet pickup.

recruiting more sponsor interest, plans were being made for a companion event—the Baja 500. This shorter race takes its competitors on a difficult swing from the seacoast inland through desert and mountains and back to where they started, roughly 558 miles and several thousand agonizing bumps earlier. Although the Baja 500, held each June, has never quite achieved the international status of its big brother, it is a definite bruiser and many top competitors insist it is a much tougher race.

"You're going over rougher terrain in the 500," explained Johnny Johnson, an off-road veteran who has won his dune buggy class in both races. "A lot of the mileage in the 1000 is over fairly decent road. But most of the course in the 500 is dirt trail and you can't even see where you're going."

But off-road racers will always follow the action, no matter how rough. One of the most torturous events is a 400-miler staged each March in Las Vegas, Nevada, by the International Desert Racing Association. The IDRA and NORRA are the two largest and most successful groups conducting races, but literally dozens of small clubs hold regular and popular events throughout the Southwest. None of these smaller events compare in glamour or profit to the Big Three, of course, but they do offer off-road enthusiasts a chance to compete on a regular basis. And that, after all, is still what off-road racing is supposed to be about.

Many dune buggy and four-wheel-drive vehicle events are actually conducted on closed courses which still offer the challenges that drivers and fans enjoy in open events. At the same time they give spectators including crews, wives and girl friends, a chance to watch the action. These closed courses, at least the better ones, combine most of the elements found in true desert racing—hills, jumps, hard dirt, soft sand and even mud holes or streams.

Some of these meets, like the annual Four-Wheel-Drive Grand Prix in Riverside (not at the International Raceway), enjoy considerable success in attracting both entries and spectators. The concentric course at Riverside includes rough dirt, soft sand and a river bed among its obstacles. Two vehicles are run at a time. One starts on the outer course and the other on the inner portion of the circuit. As they complete one lap, they switch courses for a second and final lap. A day's racing consists of a series of two-car eliminations, just as in drag racing.

Most such events, however, rarely bring out more than a hundred or so spectators, and most of these are family and friends. Off-road racing, at least in these formative years, isn't proving to be a spectator sport. It seems that its growing band of followers want a piece of the action, rather than content themselves with sitting on the sidelines swilling beer in the warm sun while cheering their heroes onward. This is a fact that a few eager promoters learned the hard way. Regular weekly races at Ascot Park, in Gardena, California, bombed after a brief season during which the promoter tired of seeing more faces in the pits than in the stands.

Other closed-course events have succeeded, however, and with the growing popularity of off-road vehicles the number of events staged each weekend for the benefit of enthusiasts continues to increase on a trial-and-error basis. There is also a growing trend toward separation of vehicles according to type. Some folks view this with a jaundiced eye while others merely see it as normal evolution. The annual Labor Day weekend bash at Pismo Beach in California is a good example. This highly successful event staged by the California Association of Four Wheel Drive Clubs, is for Jeeps, Broncos and similar machines, exclusively. Dozens of sand buggies will show up for the event, but they are brought there by their owners to play in the sand with. The sponsoring organization does not invite them to join in the formal competition. Motorcycles are being excluded more and more in off-road competition by sponsoring clubs. The two major Baja races, the Mexican 1000 and the Baja 500, are about the only significant events where two-wheelers compete at the same time, albeit in a separate class, as the four-wheel machinery.

"It makes sense," said one Southern California buggy driver who has had a hand in organizing several club-style events. "We don't have anything against bike riders, but we run these events for fun, not profit. It's a club event for cars. We want to keep the competition simple so everyone can have fun, that's our reason for existing."

Not everyone takes that view, however. "I think it's a shame," said one veteran Baja cyclist. "A lot of bike riders have worked hard to help get off-road racing together, and now we're being shut out."

Many motorcycle riders don't care, however. They say that most courses today, including the Baja runs, are becoming too fast and smooth to be challenging. These riders are, instead, turning to motocross racing or buggies.

Indeed, off-road racing is turning increasingly to smaller courses in prescribed areas, or (*horrors*) to the *pavement*! Many clubs, and even larger bodies like NORRA and IDRA, frequently hold what they call "Bug-Ins" and "Buggy Bashes" at drag strips and on parking lots. Among the events are, believe it or not, drag races and slaloms. Where terrain and facilities permit, the clubs also offer obstacle courses which, with a little imagination, can be considered off-road-style events. Such meets, however plastic they may seem to purists, are growing in frequency and popularity—especially in large, sprawling urban areas like Los Angeles where rugged terrain can be a long ride from home.

So from cramped, paved parking lots in suburban shopping centers, to the dusty and bumpy trails of Baja California, off-road racing is flourishing in one form or another, at least for now. But this youngest member of the motorsports family lacks the solid organization and guidance that some of its cousins such as sports car and drag racing enjoy and thrive on. It also is being attacked by ecologists who fume that buggies and motorcycles roaring across the countryside are destroying plant and animal life. In fact the future of off-road racing may be more in the hands of state and federal officials than it is in club members and other interested followers. On August 9, 1972, the federal government dealt off-road racing a blow that left the sport's followers stunned and staggering. On that day J. R. Penny, California director for the federal Bureau of Land Management, said that—effective immediately—no organized off-road vehicle events involving twenty-five or more such vehicles would be allowed in the desert without a special land-use permit. The ruling was viewed in some quarters as spelling doom to off-road racing. But most followers, however disgruntled, recognized the action as inevitable and immediately set to work mapping new strategy for their events.

"People think of the desert in Southern California as stern and tough," Penny said in discussing the action. "But it's fragile and must be protected."

Penny said the requirement of a land-use permit is a follow-up to President Nixon's order that public lands be protected from environmental insults. He said off-road vehicle events pose a major environmental threat to desert areas. "That's because there are a lot of vehicles involved and they are used in a competitive fashion," Penny said. "They are either races, involving machines such as motorcycles, or rallies. Such activities can cause a lot of damage."

The number of such events doubled in 1971 from the previous

year. In 1971 there were more than 150 off-road events involving some 60,000 motorcycles and four-wheel vehicles on federal public land in California. The vast majority of these events were in desert areas east of Los Angeles and San Diego.

"We aren't opposed to such activities," Penny said. "But we want to make sure that they are held in proper areas and efficiently managed to avoid damage."

Now when people want to hold mass off-road vehicle activities they must apply for the land-use permits from the bureau's agencies. A standard ten-dollar fee is charged for the permit itself. A rental fee also is levied for the use of government land.

"We have been told by our attorney that we can't allow use of the land without charging a fee," Penny said. "Without charging a fee we are, in effect, giving a gift of the land to some people. We would be breaking the law."

In addition to paying a rental fee, sponsors of events are required to put up money in bond form guaranteeing to repay the government for any damage to land and resources which may occur. Those obtaining permits are required to clearly mark the course the vehicles will use, confine the vehicles to the course and clean up all litter and route markers after the event. Penny said the permits will be issued only if "the event is held in a place we feel won't be damaged and if it's going to be carried on in a way which won't harm the area."

Next target of the government will be damage caused by off-road vehicles which aren't part of scheduled events. They include motorcycles, dune buggies, trail bikes and four-wheel-drive vehicles used in desert areas by individuals and families on weekend outings. "In the future we are going to designate areas where use of such vehicles will be banned and where they will be permitted," Penny said. "We also will set down rules under which they can be used on federal land."

But despite rigid controls in California, off-road racing rolls on unabated in Mexico, the place where the seeds of great stories are planted in the cruel and primitive wilderness, and blossom days later over a cold beer in the back of somebody's camper.

2 THE ALL-NIGHT CARNIVAL

Baja California has often been described as the earth's appendix. You have to see it to fully understand why, but the unflattering reference is not wholly unjustified. The interior is largely uninhabited, hostile and untouched. The population is dispersed along the east and west coasts, clustered into small villages and towns that seem primitive and untouched by the twentieth century. The landscape is a montage of rocks, brush-covered hills, usually dry washes (after a rainstorm they turn into raging little rivers too treacherous to cross), thick scrub brush and eerie-looking 50-foot-high spines of cacti dotting the gnarled terrain. During the day, particularly in the summer months, temperatures often climb to more than 120 degrees in some areas. At night, almost any time of the year, the thermometer drops drastically and chilled winds hurry in from the Pacific Ocean followed by thick banks of white ooze called fog. The rattlesnake population far outnumbers its human counterpart. Water is scarce in some places, nonexistent in others. If this sounds like a generally miserable and hostile place in which to spend much time, congratulations, the message is getting through! Baja California is bad news for anyone except the very hardy and/or foolish. Just the right ingredients for off-road racing and the madcap band of folks who indulge in this increasingly popular pastime.

Twice a year, in June and again in November, several thousand *norteamericanos* venture into this primitive wonderland for races that have captured the imagination of folks penned into a much more modern and convenient mode of living. A world of freeways, television, comfortable automobiles, paved streets, telephones, air-conditioned restaurants—all the little luxuries that Baja California doesn't offer. They come in campers, pickup trucks, psychedelic-painted vans, expensive sports cars, metallic-colored Detroit cars pulling big fancy trailers with conveniences most Baja Californians never heard of, on motorcycles and even by thumb with knapsacks strapped on bare, sun-bronzed backs.

Off-road racing in Baja California is probably the only sporting event where the participants miss most of the fun. While the modern gladiators are bouncing through the deserts and mountains at breakneck speed and biting the baby-powder-fine dust, their wives, sweethearts, friends, neighbors and fans keep a festive vigil spirited by booze and song.

To a motorsports buff, Baja California at race time has all the charisma of a Woodstock music festival—only the sounds people listen to most are the ear-splitting crackle of a motorcycle, the high-pitched whine of a VW-powered dune buggy or the deep rumble of a Ford Bronco V8. The whole scene is a giant love-in for a cult that worships horsepower and speed instead of grass and hard rock. This is where Mr. and Mrs. Middle America forget their suburban ethic and show the world they too know how to have fun.

Both Baja races start in Ensenada, a usually placid little seaport town some 65 miles below the border. Off-road racing is big busi-

Three hundred dune buggies and desert racers parade through downtown Las Vegas past Mint Hotel race headquarters. Parade marks the beginning of the Mint 400 each year, and attracts multitudes of curious spectators and entertainment celebrities.

ness in Baja. Emilio Méndez Aguirre, director of tourism in Ensenada, estimates more than 10,000 *americanos* converge on that community of 36,000 for each race. Hotel rooms—there are roughly 1500 in Ensenada—are always booked solid months in advance. Even some VIPs, such as clean-cut representatives from American Motors and the Ford Motor Company, have to make arrangements to bunk with pit crews in campers and trailers parked along the beach and in vacant lots near the impound area where nearly 300 vehicles wait for the action. Hundreds of U.S. visitors, many of whom come south only to join the fun and be able to say "they were there," curl up on the nearby beach under flimsy blankets and in shabby sleeping bags. Most of their warmth comes not from the smoldering fires and wraps, but from the half-empty bottles of rum and tequila resting in the sand.

"Man, I couldn't afford a hotel room if there was one," said one hefty motorcycle vagabond. He pointed absently to a greasy sleeping bag lashed to his motorcycle. "That's my home, dad. It's enough for me."

But whether they arrive carrying sleeping bags or a cache of credit cards, the *americanos* pump more than half a million dollars into the Ensenada economy each year. "We do three to four months' business in just four days," said Rodolfo Núñez, a clerk at the liquor store near the start/finish line and pit area. "Last year we took in more than $15,000 during the race. Our usual business is about $1000 a week."

Hotels and restaurants triple and quadruple the number of meals they serve. One restaurant manager said he ordered enough food during one race invasion to last a month under normal circumstances, but he still ended up running out of several popular entrees, such as steak before the crowd left town. No one complains, except when the weather plays cruel tricks, as it did in November 1972. Baja California is frequently battered by hurricane winds and heavy rainstorms that rip up the already rugged terrain and leave it in even worse condition than usual (although many Baja buffs find that hard to imagine). The 1972 Mexican 1000 was started in Mexicali instead of Ensenada. Mexicali, the capital of Baja California, is located some 120 miles inland from the Pacific Ocean near the U.S./Mexico border. The new route added some 80 miles to the overall distance, and took racers south from Mexicali 85 miles to El Paraíso on the Gulf of California, then inland across the mountains and desert to Camalú on the Pacific Coast. From there the race followed its traditional pattern. In both the Baja 500 and the Mexican 1000 drivers are required to stop at each checkpoint along the way. What they do or where they go in between is their business, but if they don't hit all the checkpoints, and have their card marked, even Melvin Belli couldn't succeed in defending their case to NORRA officials in La Paz.

The route for the 1972 Mexican 1000, like its predecessors, was mostly sand, silt, rocks, mud, salt and water. As usual more than half of the entries in the punishing race never made it down the peninsula to La Paz. A hurricane a few weeks earlier had taken its toll on the main highway south out of Mexicali. In spots the road abruptly disappeared. Blotto. Nothing but sand and rocks and detour signs pointing the way. Flooded houses, flooded cars, deserted restaurants and roadside graves were eerie reminders of the past. Dune buggies roared by kicking up clouds of powdery dust and weaving along through the debris. Nothing much survived the storm, it seemed, but the tall cacti stretching skyward like spearpoints of a vegetable army. But as the racers headed southward they brought with them new life. Small bands of Mexicans, perhaps left homeless by the devastating storm, found their way to a hilltop to watch the excitement. They don't know why these crazy *gringos* would want to come here to do this, but they're glad nevertheless. It is a temporary diversion. Even some of those *gringos* who chose to enter this motor mayhem can't explain why.

"We're all nuts to do this, aren't we?" said Bruce Korstad as he revved the engine of his $5000 dune buggy built especially for the race. "I just bought this engine and this is the first time I've had it on any highway. So I decided to take it to Baja and the One Thousand. Why? I guess it's the old 'because it's there' bit. Oh, I don't expect to finish the race, just get in my licks."

Korstad and his partner Peter Lafferty are from Eugene, Oregon. Their wives are AWOL elementary school teachers who "got sick" that week in time for the 1000. Since its inception in 1967, the *Mil Millas de México* has become an international classic, and attracts such rally and racing stars as Swedish driver Erik Carlsson, who swears the race is the toughest in the world—even worse than the treacherous and demanding East African Safari rally. Only about the first 90 and the last 130 miles of the 1000 are on paved road. The course is so rough that all steering and suspension components have to be wired to avoid being vibrated off along the way. The dust trail kicked up by cars and even motorcycles makes visibility almost zero if you're within 200 yards of another vehicle. At one point along the misery trail it is nearly a half hour quicker to drive along the beach than to follow the more direct inland route, even though the beach trip is 20 miles longer.

The best prepared and rehearsed teams always have alternate

routes in case conditions at race time make the preferred course slower or tougher. Sometimes that backfires, however. One year during the 1000 a buggy driver decided to avoid all the pounding, dust and heavy traffic that awaited him inland, and headed for the smooth beach sand. But when he arrived at the shore it was not only high tide, but the fog made any kind of movement faster than five miles an hour insanely dangerous. The driver decided to head back inland and take his lumps, but the detour cost him nearly an hour of precious time and killed any chance he ever had of finishing in the money.

Drivers are permitted to pick their own routes, so long as they stop in at each of the eight or so designated checkpoints. Pre-running the course prior to the race itself is almost a must for anyone seriously expecting to finish with a high position. But even that doesn't always prove fruitful. Unexpected rainstorms, fog and high winds can radically change driving conditions and even alter the terrain enough at times to get experienced drivers like Andy DeVercelly and Johnny Johnson temporarily lost. Think what would happen, in fact does happen, each year to dozens of neophyte racers blundering blissfully along. And, of course, if you don't make it, what then? Like the guys who deserted their buggy at Felix Mendoza's garage and disappeared into the night stocked with beer, some drivers figure it's not worth the trouble salvaging their equipment. Sometimes they simply can't work out any arrangements for several days or weeks, and when they do return—nothing. No sign of the buggy or motorcycle they left several days earlier. There aren't any accurate figures available from either NORRA or the Mexican government, but there undoubtedly are enough buggy and motorcycle parts scattered throughout Baja California to keep local residents in transportation for a long time if they could put them all together.

A focal point of the action each year in the Mexican 1000 is El Arco. A dusty, weather-worn little town about halfway down the peninsula, it serves as the driver and rider change point, repair headquarters for pit crews and round-the-clock party center for family, friends and fans of those bounding through the wilderness.

When the sun goes down in El Arco, the residents usually take the hint and call it a day. Except, of course, during the 1000. This is something they wouldn't want to miss—even if they *could* sleep. So they watch, in a sort of bemused silence.

The only light in town seems to come from a string of colored light bulbs strung across the road at the checkpoint. There is a table nearby, and officials with stopwatches and clipboards wait for the racers to arrive in town. Despite the distant sounds of music and laughing, it is quiet in El Arco. And cold, very cold. A crowd of *gringos*, maybe thirty or forty strong, stands by the plaza fountain in the chilly night air . . . waiting . . . listening. One of them, a guy with an Australian jungle hat, is carrying a bleach bottle. Every few minutes he puts it to his lips and drinks. He won't say what's in the plastic container, but his offer to let anyone else share usually passes without much interest. (Later in the night, as the chill penetrates the bones and leaves them aching, folks will accept his offer heartily.) But Funny Hat doesn't care, he just takes enthusiastic slugs and then wipes his mouth with the back of his hand—just like in the movies. He is wearing a T-shirt with "Coors —Breakfast of Champions" stenciled on the front. His bulging muscles stretch the sleeves, and one member of the crowd comments that "from the looks of him, maybe that really is bleach." But Funny Hat is really just having fun, and wanting others to share in his pleasure.

On each side of the one-lane dirt road leading through the *pueblo* are tents, scores of them. The tents are instant garages, hastily erected by pit crews who know that their racers will be hurting when they roll through the checkpoint. Some of the canvas garages are elaborate: chain hoists, spare parts and even welding torches that work off droning two-cycle generators. The pit crews sit in front of their tents, drinking beer, talking, waiting.

Anticipation grows and the mood in El Arco is increasingly restless. The first contestant should be arriving *any minute*. Someone turns up the jukebox or portable radio, whatever it is. Coffee is still the most popular beverage at this point in the evening, but when the tension breaks and the first few vehicles pull into town and

Pit area in Ensenada prior to either the Baja 500 or Mexican 1000 is always a favorite spot for fans and camera bugs. In this shot actor/race driver James Garner draws attention as he chats with a lady friend.

then roar off into the unknown darkness, bottles of rum and tequila will begin to appear, passing from hand to hand. Then sounds of hammering, drilling and shouting will join the chorus of dune buggy and motorcycle engines.

Suddenly there's a stampede toward the checkpoint. Under the string of colored light bulbs, the first racer has arrived, a battered and wobbling dune buggy so covered with dust it looks as if it was sprayed with baby powder. The drivers, slowly and stiffly climbing out, look like a pair of Egyptian mummies with goggles.

"Who is it?" asks someone on the outer edges of the crowd.

"Hell if I can tell," says a companion. "Too many people, I can't see the number."

Activity is beginning to pick up now, a new mood fills the night air and somehow it seems a little warmer. The crowd jams in around the two drivers as they gulp down Gatorade and splash water in their eyes from a cup someone handed them. Everyone wants to ask a question: How's the route? Have you seen so-and-so? Is What's-his-name still working on that broken axle back at the checkpoint in Rancho Santa Ynez? Did Whoosits ever fix that busted A-frame a few miles north of here? The drivers try to answer each question between gulps. Meanwhile the pit crew moves the car to a tent and hurriedly begins checking this, tightening that, and filling it with gasoline. Tires are changed. One guy, who looks important, asks the drivers certain questions about the car and they answer in sober tones. He seems concerned but satisfied with their answers and turns back to the crew to double check their work. A couple of more gulps of Gatorade and the duo are back in their machine and racing out of town. Somehow they leave a sense of loneliness and envy behind them in a roostertail of white dust.

As the eastern sky turns bright crimson, Funny Hat is still sipping from the plastic bleach bottle—only now he has some company. Among them is an attractive young woman with a fancy beauty-shop coiffure that is beginning to show signs of wear. She sips gingerly from the bottle in turn and chain smokes long filtered cigarettes. Earlier in the evening she was worried because her hus-

Upwards of 10,000 fans usually line the main street of Ensenada each
year for the start of both the Baja 500 in June and the Mexican 1000
in November. With buggies, pickup trucks, four-wheel-drive rigs and
motorcycles all leaving at one-minute intervals it requires more than
four hours to get everyone rolling and out of town.

band was overdue. But someone, maybe it was a motorcycle rider, said he saw the car sidelined with a broken driveshaft. Now Mrs. Fancy Hair is relieved and starting to have fun, waiting for her husband to finally make it to El Arco before they head back home.

The crowd has thinned considerably by now, though. Sleeping bags are everywhere—beside buildings, in yards, in the back of trucks and under them. From somewhere the aroma of fresh coffee drifts across the dusty plaza. Across the street from the fountain is a barn-like adobe building with a freshly painted sign out front saying: El Arco Hilton. Inside, the "Hilton" is wall-to-wall sleeping bags except for a corner near the door where an enterprising member of the community is selling Mexican beer from a broken refrigerator at twenty-five cents a can—he has plenty of customers. *"Cerveza, por favor"* appears to be a favorite expression of *norteamericanos* in El Arco tonight.

Local residents, still awed by the show, sit quietly and serenely on the sidelines outside their adobe houses. Here and there children play and watch the confusion and no one bugs them about it being past their bedtime. After all, there are no movie houses or television around here, and the 1000 is the biggest event of the year. It's the circus and Fourth of July all rolled into a few hours of confusion.

But despite the carnival-like atmosphere that trails off-road racers, this is still a no-nonsense business. Those few who take it lightly are quickly left behind. There are two major stumbling blocks confronting the adventurer who finally decides to give Baja a go. One is choosing the path that is least likely to tear up his—or her—equipment, yet leads to the finish line. The other is combatting the elements. Washouts and rocks that make up most of the route are great for tearing the suspension right out from under even some of the most solid and well-prepared machines. Sharp rocks will cut tires and that notorious powdery dust gets into *every*thing.

Dust is the sneakiest hazard racers must guard against. For both themselves (it even creeps under goggles) and their equipment. "You don't know it has struck until after it has done its damage," explained veteran off-roader Dave Ekins. What happens is that dust, finer than baby powder, works its way into the engine and electrical system. Johnny Johnson estimates that sand and dust ruin more Baja efforts than any other single enemy the off-road racer faces. When this happens it is called "sanding the engine" by Baja buffs—it spells many dollars and lots of hard work to correct.

But while Baja California is rough and demanding on both men and equipment, it doesn't necessarily have a corner on that sort of ingredient. Several hundred miles north, in the drab, lifeless Nevada desert near Las Vegas, is one of the toughest races on the map: the Mint 400. Held each year in March, this race regularly attracts all the top names in off-road racing, and perhaps even more show business and professional driving types then either of the Baja events. It is a tortuous trek that originally consisted of eight exhausting laps around a fifty-mile course. About the only civilized aspect of the Mint 400 is the time of year race director Mel Larson picked to run the event. The desert sun is just warm enough in March to permit shirt sleeves during daylight hours, and the starlight nights are usually pleasant enough to demand nothing more than a light jacket at most. But the niceties end there abruptly.

As Los Angeles *Times* sports writer Shav Glick aptly put it: "Mel Larson isn't a junk car dealer, but the way he lays out the course for the Mint 400 you'd think he was. Or at least wanted to become one."

Of course Larson only smiles mischievously when he hears such talk. It means he's done his job well. When the three days of dueling with the desert is finished, the course is strewn with the broken carcasses of motorcycles, dune buggies, trucks, Jeeps and even many of the support vehicles. The reasons, naturally, are pretty much the same old Baja song: dust, jagged rocks, steep inclines and tortuous miles of dips, chuckholes and tough old desert brush.

The race starts and ends in front of the Mint Gun Club located about a dozen miles outside of town. Anyone heading in that direction during the day won't have any trouble locating the course, a cloud of reddish brown dust floats across the desert the entire length of the exhaustive loop. The narrow paved road off the main highway to the club is lined with campers, street buggies, air-conditioned Cadillacs, expensive foreign and domestic sports cars—the same colorful array of vehicles you usually find in Ensenada around June or November. Strangely familiar in fact, it doesn't even look as if they've been washed since you saw them last. Inside the gun club, which serves as race and press headquarters, is a bar, short-order grill and plenty of slot machines and gambling tables. Everything is in use. The race plays no favorites, and much of the top talent is out of the running early. Parnelli Jones, knocked out of the race with a broken drive shaft in his Stroppe-prepared Bronco, sips a drink as he watches his attractive wife Judy try her hand at blackjack. The cards are coming her way today, and Parnelli is obviously pleased that the family luck isn't all bad. But just to be on the safe side he declines an offer to join in and instead opts for a refill.

Across the room, leaning languidly against the bar and sipping beer from a paper cup, actor James Garner chats with two newspapermen about his racing adventures. He is dressed in a driving suit and his face, except for the outline of where the goggles were, is covered with powdery white dust. Even his curly black hair is snow white. Things didn't go well for Garner this day. His powerful Vic Hickey-prepared Oldsmobile Banshee, a Cutlass model converted for off-road competition, collided with another car in the blinding dust storm the racers churn up. Garner is out of the competition despite frantic efforts by his pit crew to repair the disabled machine. This man who earns his living by that sturdy-looking chiseled face took a bump on the jaw in the collision.

"This is by far the toughest course I've competed on," he tells the reporters. "And it's tough because you never really know where in the hell you're at out there half the time.

"A lot of these guys just haul buns around the course and don't think about that until they plow into somebody."

Garner is obviously irritated at what happened to him. He was sure he had a good chance this time of placing high in the standings —maybe even scoring a class victory. But somebody did a job on him and crushed another dream. Does he think the course should be altered to make it a little more realistic? one of the reporters asks. "Hell, no, man!" he replies excitedly. "This is their race. Let

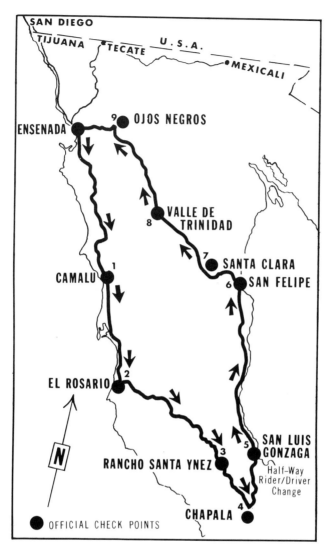

Shows route followed by racers on Baja 500, including checkpoints as indicated by dark dots. Course follows 558-mile trek through mountains and desert.

'em run it the way they see fit."

Garner then puzzles for a while as he sips a fresh brew. "I would like to see them put some kind of limit on the number of entries, however," he says thoughtfully. "Or maybe be a little discriminating about who enters. There are some guys out there who I don't think should be out there. I just don't know . . ."

The crowd stirs and surges toward the doorway. Mickey Thompson, covered with dust, steps into the room looking glum. He crosses to the bar, nods to Garner and the two reporters and orders a beer. The crowd gathers around Thompson to find out what happened to him. The race is less than half over but already about half of the field is out of the running.

The Mint 400 is one of the races where motorcycles run seprately, and the two-wheelers seem to like it that way for obvious reasons. They don't kick up the dust the four-wheel vehicles do, hence it's easier to see where you're going and breathe at the same time. It is also one helluva lot safer. Partly because of Mel Larson's savvy (he's an accomplished stock car and road racer) the race attracts more than one hundred motorcycles each year, nearly three times the number that enter the Baja events. Larson, naturally simpático with the drivers and riders, listens to their complaints and suggestions. For the 1972 race he decided to alter the course, adding a couple of high-speed runs to go along with usually rugged terrain. Instead of the traditional eight trips around a 50-mile lap, racers now follow a 67-mile loop for six circles. The extra distance (the total race is now two miles longer) will now include both a six-mile high-speed paved section and another six-mile high-speed graded road area. Some of the very rough backstretch region that competitors legitimately groaned about in the past has been eliminated. Larson said the new configuration will make the race more competitive than ever, giving the big-bore machines (such as the Broncos), which in the past were getting waxed by smaller, less powerful but more nimble cars, an even better shot at winning.

Unlike the Baja contests, viewing the Mint race is quite possible if you don't mind getting dirty. It is important, however, to be very careful if you decide to strike out across the desert to take in some of the action. In the past there have been incidents where confused spectators wandered onto the course by accident and created instant panic and confusion, but fortunately no serious accidents resulted. Larson now has the course clearly marked and guarded to prevent this, but it is still necessary to pay attention, especially at night.

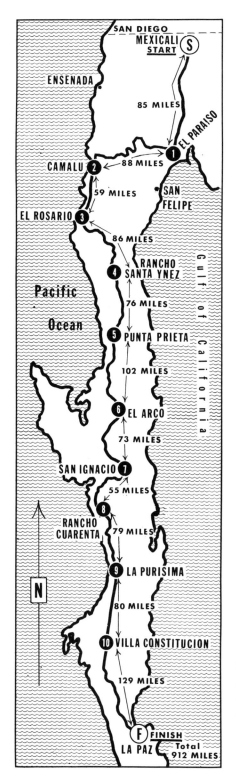

This map shows latest 912-mile route of Mexican 1000 from Mexicali to La Paz. Fog, wind and rain often hamper contestants.

Even the racers themselves sometimes get disoriented in the dark and dust. One year a buggy driver wound up on his head in a ditch nearly a mile from the course, unhurt but very, very unhappy. It took nearly an hour to tow him out of the mess and send him on his way.

Larson is also aware of the critical view the federal government is taking of such activity. Working carefully and patiently with the U.S. Bureau of Land Management, state and county officials and private land owners, Larson developed what has become known as the safest and "cleanest" off-road race of its kind anywhere. Clean in this case refers not to the huge clouds of dust churned up by racers, but rather that competitors follow a clearly defined route, which is pretty much restricted to dry washes.

Further, to prevent the thought from germinating in anyone's mind that some kind of shortcut across the desert might be a clever idea, checkpoint stations have been strategically placed. To back them up, patrols constantly rove on land and in the air to check the progress of the race. Although off-road racing *a la* Baja may continue in its present format, such events in the United States are obviously going to be forced to follow the example of the Mint operation, like it or not.

There are obvious safety advantages to closed course events. If a serious accident does occur it takes only minutes for medical help to arrive at the scene, via either helicopter or land vehicle. Nearby first-aid stations and local hospitals also add up in the plus column. This isn't to say that NORRA is in anyway negligent about its responsibilities to the racers, but medical facilities are scarce in Baja and in case of serious injury minutes can make a big difference. NORRA always maintains a volunteer air patrol while the race is in progress. But accidents don't always happen where it's convenient for a fixed-wing aircraft to land. Again the time element.

Another advantage to the closed course event is easier scoring, although keeping tabs on an off-road race is a statistician's nightmare. Not so anymore in Las Vegas. The Mint Hotel and Casino, which sponsors the annual meet, has invested $500,000 in a computer to get that job done quickly and accurately.

When you're trying to keep track of some 400 entries of various sizes and shapes, all bounding about there in the dust, somehow a pencil and a pad of paper just doesn't seem to cut it. In previous years the battery of race statisticians remained suspended in a state of absolute frenzy from the handing out of starting assignments through the rugged race itself. They had to keep track of the fortunes and failings of every single entry with only the help of two-way radios and aerial spotters. Unavoidably there were more than a few errors, and results, at best, were slow in coming (a situation that unfortunately continues in Baja events). After the dust settled and the throngs of participants and spectators made their way to the gambling tables and lounges, the exhausted and frustrated statisticians were just beginning their toughest job—sorting out the results. This usually took up to twelve bleary-eyed hours. But now the computer, an IBM Systems III Model 10, which was introduced at the 1972 Mint race, does all the work from beginning to end— and does it accurately.

"Use of the computer will cut down any chance for errors that can crop up to delay figuring of the final results," said Larson. "It will also save a lot of headaches and frustration and get the job done much quicker."

The computer begins its racing day by assembling a complete entry list that includes starting positions and the many different vehicle categories. As the race progresses it will digest tidbits of information fed it by spotters from around the course and spit out answers immediately. Almost before the last car rolls up to the finish line the computer has a complete rundown of the results— from the first dropout to the last finisher.

It isn't likely that we'll see computers at every off-road race in the near future, however. Not many, if any, promoters or organizations have the financial backing that comes with the Sahara-Nevada Corporation, owner of the Mint Hotel and sponsor of the Mint 400. But this race does demonstrate how far the sport has come in the past few years from that first dash up some sand dune with a can of cold beer awaiting the winner.

3 A GAME THE WHOLE FAMILY CAN PLAY

————————————————————————————→

When it comes to that burgeoning craze called off-road racing, the name Tom Small isn't exactly synonymous with, say, the likes of Parnelli Jones or Mickey Thompson. Unless you happen to be talking about Tom Small stories.

In the lobby of the Hotel Lucerna in Mexicali the night before the start of the 1972 Mexican 1000, Tom Small was the favorite topic of discussion. For instance there was the preceding year's race when Small ran out of gas as he was charging down the 832-mile trek from Ensenada to La Paz. Not just once—but five times.

Not to be outdone this particular year, Small wanted to make sure everything was fitting and proper, so two weeks before the big event he decided to get the jump on everyone by running the entire new 912-mile course from Mexicali to La Paz. It turned out to be another almost perfect trip. Almost. When Small returned to Mexicali he was informed by some sheepish soul that he had gone the wrong way. Ouch!

Ready for more? Small had to mooch gas off a pair of honeymooners one year. Another case of not finding the corner service station in time. In November 1971, during the fifth annual edition of the notorious Mexican 1000, the entire gas tank on Small's desert buggy split open from a bad welding job.

But Small, using the ingenuity that drivers in this roughed up bit of racing are known for, borrowed a bait tank off one of the fishing boats at Punta Prieta and loaded it with fuel.

Actually Small, a thirty-year-old National City, California, electrician, isn't really all thumbs. It's just that this exercise has a habit of making fools out of some of the world's best racers.

But Tom Small stories seem to offer that special twist. Despite his hard luck, Small managed a fifth-place finish in 1971, good enough for a slice of the purse. He reportedly invested in some gasoline. But his confusion about finding the right course on his pre-run fiasco is understandable.

There are various ways to get to La Paz. Small took a path which, as he soon found out, had been termed impassable due to severe hurricane damage to the things they call roads in Baja California. While Small and a few of his buddies were on this pre-run, Mexican 1000 officials quietly changed the route of the 1972 race. The new route headed out of Mexicali, traveled 88 miles south toward San Felipe on the coast of the Gulf of California, before turning inland on a roughed-up mountain trail to San Vicente. Then on to Camalú and the old race route.

Small liked his way better, especially after he spent two and a half days repairing a 70-foot hole in one road south of San Felipe.

"It took us almost three days piling rocks, one by one, in this huge ditch, before we could cross it," said Small. "That part of the road is passable now thanks to our great engineering work."

Tom Small, like every other hardy member of the off-road fraternity, takes his lumps good-naturedly. But why off-road racing

*James Garner signs an au-
tograph just before start of
1972 Baja 500 in Ensenada,
and then hams it up some
for the fans.*

anyway for an ordinary, unpublicized, middle class man like Tom Small? There are the obvious stock answers. The lure of freedom and adventure. No cops. No stop signals or rules. No Sunday drivers (well, not as *many!*). But Small says he needs something else. Competition. That he finds plenty of in off-road events—wherever he finds them.

When he graduated from high school in 1960, Small had a football scholarship to the University of Southern California in his hip pocket. As a beefy and aggressive center for his high school team he had impressed the guys at USC. But a bad motorcycle accident, one which severely injured his neck and spine, put him out of sports such as football for good.

"I still needed something, so I turned to racing," said Small. "It was just three years ago. I didn't know zilch about cars. Didn't even know what a carburetor was. But I found out."

In the weeks of preparation leading up to the Mexican 1000, Small has taken time off from his job so he could be locked in his garage working over every nut and bolt on his Funco buggy.

"It would only take one loose nut to put you out of this race," he said. "The race is won or lost in the garage."

Small, who incidentally weighs in at 240 pounds and stands five feet eleven inches tall, said he spends close to $12,500 getting ready for the big race. Some of the funds come from his sponsor, a Texas mobile-home maker. The winner's share in his class is only $3000. Obviously not very good business, right?

Perhaps not. But Small, like most other off-road racers, is motivated by other ambitions.

"I'm not in it for money," he explained. "Racing isn't my livelihood and I wasn't even going to enter the race anymore after last year. I had the car sitting up on blocks. But then . . ."

Tom Small's story could be repeated several hundred times for nearly all but a handful of the men and women who enter off-road races from Las Vegas to Baja California.

Women? That's right. Amid the grubby bustle of the pits, they look strangely out of place. Chic, exotic, gentle women race drivers.

But put a gas pedal under their painted toes and a gear shift between their manicured fingernails and they suddenly strike a threatening pose. Hold on to your distributor caps, gang, the he-man Mexican 1000—that granddaddy of motor mayhem south of the border—is sexually integrated. No sexists, those NORRA folks!

Yep. Women drivers. The same breed that holds up traffic in the fast lane during rush hour, the same Oh-I'm-sorry-I-forgot-to-signal beauties, have invaded this manly stronghold. So much so that in the 1972 Mexican 1000 at least a half dozen girls, most of them *Playboy* centerfold material in their twenties, took off into the wilds confident they could even *win* the tortuous race to La Paz. None did. But some did finish.

It's another case of that old story about beauty and the beast. Lovely and shapely females rubbing elbows with greasy veteran male drivers of the off-road circuit. Only somehow in the crazy whirlwind world of this infant sport it seems so *natural*. You have to really *think* about it before it begins to seem odd, and it has nothing to do with women's liberation.

"I need women's lib like Beverly Hills needs a poverty program," said Kim Bryce, of Huntington Beach, California, as she prepared to roar off southward. Kim said she has been hanging around spare parts and oily garages ever since she can remember. She could handle a wrench before she learned how to work a lipstick.

"I'm not a tomboy," she said. "I just love racing and cars. I started working in the pits at these races, then I talked a sponsor into letting me drive a car."

Most sponsors would shudder at the thought of putting a young (twenty-one) female without much experience into a $5000 machine headed south in the toughest race of its kind. But Kim had some pull, so to speak. Her sponsor turned out to be Dr. Bill Bryce, her father. That's off-road racing.

"I just told Daddy I could handle the job and he finally let me go," Kim said.

Helen Clements, twenty-four, and a former model, broke into the game running errands for mechanics near her home in Van

Nuys, a Los Angeles suburb. But she has definite thoughts about the sport.

"I don't like the greasy part of it, but I like the fun," Helen said just before speeding out of Mexicali in a Toyota. "It's a neat feeling, sliding off a road sideways, like skiing down a slope. I'm hooked."

But Helen resents many of the girls suddenly rushing into the sport. "Most of them are real jerks," she said. "They come here more for the guys and the attention than to race. They just sit around and look pretty. They don't know how to race."

But not all the ladies in off-road racing are fledgling leadfoots. Both Paula Murphy, often billed as the "fastest woman on wheels," and Pat Moss Carlsson, sister of former Grand Prix driving star Stirling Moss and wife of rally king Erik Carlsson, have tried their hand in either the Baja events or the Mint race in Las Vegas.

Paula, an attractive brunette from Granada Hills, California, was the first woman to drive a jet car at Bonneville, and set a two-way flying mile record of 226.37 mph that was later broken. She is the only woman to take a 100 mph-plus practice lap at the Indianapolis Motor Speedway, a feat she recorded in the STP Novi. In 1969 Paula scored still another feminine first when she topped the 200 mph barrier on a quarter-mile drag strip, a record that climaxed a long struggle with sanctioning agencies to gain licensing privileges for women in exotic fuel-burning funny cars. In 1971 she whistled around the high-banked Talladega, Alabama, oval at a five-lap average of 171.449 mph at the wheel of a Plymouth to claim the world closed course record for women. Paula also has competed against men in power boats, sports cars, jalopies and drag racing machines.

"I think off-road racing is a gas. All racing is fun," Paula said.

But is the off-road variety rougher than other genre?

"Yes. Definitely," she said. "I don't think it requires any more skill, exactly. No. It just takes a certain kind of stamina. You really take a beating."

There are several talented and serious-minded female drivers and even motorcycle riders in off-road racing, perhaps more than in any other motor sport going. One of the most competitive and skillful of the lot is Judy Smith, a Playa del Rey housewife and mother of two, who goes about quietly conducting her own liberation movement of sorts, and leaving a lot of disgruntled male competitors in the dust. Literally.

Judy has competed in most major off-road races in the Southwest and Mexico. In fact she not only finished the 1972 Mexican 1000 among the front runners, but drove the 912 miles down the peninsula by herself in a single-seat 2080cc VW Sandmaster dune buggy. That's an accomplishment only a handful of top gentlemen drivers can boast. But Judy is growing accustomed to such impressive feats. Earlier that same year, during the Baja 500, Judy became the first woman to finish a major off-road race alone, completing the distance in the same single-seat machine.

But despite that stirring performance, Judy did have her problems.

Early in the 500-miler the buggy developed transmission trouble not too many miles after the start and she had to nurse it most of the distance. But that wasn't all. Judy was in for still more headaches—three flat tires. The last flat she decided to ignore since she was already lost in the dark and figured she had enough to worry about just finding her way. Which she did. And soon enough to earn eleventh place in class. More than respectable considering conditions and the competition.

Judy's husband Val was a prominent desert bike rider for years, and Judy went along to the races as pit crew. Val retired from bikes a few years ago, and mazagine articles on Baja inspired the family's new interest. It wasn't long before the former two-wheel ace was ripping apart the family Volkswagen to make it ready for a Baja run. But it would be Mrs. Smith taking the wheel this time, not Val.

Judy entered the 1971 Baja 500 in the sedan class and, with her co-driver Muriel Heath, made several unsuccessful attempts to pre-run the course. Mechanical troubles with the VW turned them back each time. But it was a different story at race time. Although there were countless little mishaps and aggravating problems, the two women finished the race in 25 hours and 51 minutes

Dick Clark (with beard) and Doug Fortin (behind wheel) chat with motorsports columnist Johnny McDonald before heading out into the Baja desert. Fortin and Clark built their first racer from junked and surplus parts, and won the Baja 500 the first time they entered.

—good enough for a tenth in class and to convince Judy to keep trying.

But the majority of drivers and riders, by a margin of nearly 100 to 1, are men. Few of them are more famous than Parnelli Jones, the irrepressible former Indianapolis 500 winner who now directs his ample driving talents exclusively to off-roading.

"I won't be satisfied until I win that damned race," Jones said while chatting about the Mexican 1000. No one doubted him. Jones has never been one to equivocate on his racing goals. But his luck at that point had been less than good. Each year he would roar out of Ensenada in either the 500 or 1000 and quickly set the pace through the first two or three checkpoints, only to be eventually sidelined when the powerful Ford Bronco succumbed to the punishment.

Bill Stroppe, the man who engineered the Broncos for off-roading, always went along, riding silently at Parnelli's side in each race. In 1970, after two years of frustration, Stroppe decided to try something different.

"Parnelli is a fantastic talent," Stroppe said. "Perhaps the best in the world. And he's probably more at home on the dirt than any place else. But I don't think four-wheel-drive cars are right for him. They really can't take the sliding and drifting that Parnelli puts them through continuously."

It was that revelation that changed the record books *pronto*. In 1970 Jones and Stroppe showed up in Ensenada for the Baja 500 with a Bronco Colt, a two-wheel-drive creation featuring lightweight tube framing like the buggies, but with a fiberglass body like the Broncos and the big Ford V8 power. It proved to be the right formula, because that was the year that Parnelli broke his jinx and finished the course in a blistering 11 hours and 55 minutes.

Things didn't go so well that winter in the 1000, however. Numerous tire and axle problems bogged them down repeatedly, and it was a frustrated Parnelli who finally pulled into La Paz in no better than sixth place in his first finish in that race.

"I was so damned disgusted," Jones said candidly, "that I really didn't care that I'd finally finished. But I knew we had the right equipment now, and that I could eventually win."

He kept his word. The following year the Jones/Stroppe combo set a record of 14 hours and 59 minutes on the Ensenada to La Paz run to capture overall honors and set a record that may never be bettered. Then in 1972 the team returned to score the first back-to-back victory in the history of the Mexican 1000, making the 912-mile trip from Mexicali to La Paz in 16 hours and 47 minutes.

Jones is candid about why he drives in off-road events.

"It's sort of a novelty. I have a lot of fun out there. Besides, it gives me a chance to drive without gettting involved in a lot of legal hassles the way I would in most other racing."

And there is, of course, a practical side to Parnelli.

"It's good publicity. I want to stay active as long as I can to keep my name in print. It's good business. I know my future is in business, and that's where I'm directing most of my time and effort now. But winning a couple of big races a year is good publicity."

There are those among the off-road set who view Parnelli disapprovingly, and see him and the Stroppe-prepared Broncos as a threat to the amateur spirit of the sport. But their attitude, however honorably motivated, is about as out of date as the steam engine. Although small races, staged by clubs or individual promoters, can still dictate who enters and restrict the field to amateur types, larger groups like NORRA and IDRA welcome name drivers who add status to such races and make them more attractive to news media and sponsors.

Not all of the big-name drivers, however talented and determined, run away with the show. Mickey Thompson will testify to that fact. Probably no driver has worked harder, spent more money and had more disappointments than Thompson. And yet, like Parnelli, he insists he won't give up until he wins his share of the biggies—which usually means either the two Baja races or the Mint 400. But so far, with one or two exceptions, Mickey's experiences in off-roading have been a series of frustrations. Like most off-road racers, Thompson entered the sport first as a curious spectator.

The stocky Californian had wandered south to Ensenada in 1968 to watch the start of the second annual Mexican 1000. He said the trip was mostly motivated by his curiosity as a car builder. At least at first. Then something happened as he stood watching the buggies, Broncos, pickup trucks, VW sedans and motorcycles head out of town.

"I couldn't stand not being in there," he recalls. "I just had to try it."

He tried desperately to buy a car—any car. Thompson was so determined to be involved that he flew his own plane ahead to each checkpoint, hoping to talk his way into a ride. But that didn't work. The best he could do was help distressed drivers along the way—there were plenty of those.

The next year, 1969, Thompson was back in Ensenada, this time as a driver on the Stroppe Bronco team. But that didn't prove

Dick Russell (left) and Parnelli Jones chat with fans about their race strategy in the Baja 500. Mechanical trouble, however, ended their effort early in the race.

satisfying to a man who holds some 450 speed records and is used to winning.

"I was the last driver to join the team," he said. "So I got the leftovers. I was number six and I got number six equipment. It was to be expected, but that still didn't make me happy."

After three races Thompson decided to get his own car. He chose a Chevrolet.

"I don't get paid for driving anymore, in fact it costs me about $50,000 to go off-road racing," Thompson explained. "But now I'm preparing the equipment myself for myself."

Thompson said he picked a stock 5000-pound truck to compete against smaller, lighter vehicles because "people identify with that kind of vehicle." And sponsors like that sort of thing.

"The big thing now is off-road activity, recreation vehicles,"

Thompson said. "A pickup relates to things people are interested in now. So it seems more meaningful. Besides, they're going to sell more than a million trucks this year."

Thompson prepares his Baja vehicles in a race shop he operates in Long Beach, California, where he spends 14 to 16 hours a day working slowly, painstakingly on his equipment with his twenty-two-year-old son Danny, who also rides shotgun now in off-road events.

"I've got to win this thing," Thompson said about the Mexican 1000. "I've come so close."

Indeed he has. In the 1972 Baja 500 Thompson finished only 41 minutes behind overall winner Bob Ferro, a California dune buggy driver, in what was considered a remarkable performance for a pickup truck in a race better suited to lighter and more nimble buggies. His feat becomes even more significant at closer inspection because Thompson *lost* 47 minutes along the way while repairing a faulty transistorized ignition system. Even so he ended up third overall and second in the pickup class.

But that's not quite all. During the first two legs of that race Thompson covered the distance in exactly the same time as lead-footed Parnelli in the lightweight Bronco Colt. "We had one helluva race going on," Thompson recalls. But it fizzled when both chargers were sidelined with mechanical troubles. Thompson finally located his trouble, after a 47-minute delay. It was a loose wire.

But while the Joneses and Thompsons add a certain professional air and glamour to the scene, off-road racing is producing its own heroes and super stars. Guys like Bob Ferro, Fritz Kroyer and Johnny Johnson.

Ferro, a young Hollywood stuntman, is pegged by many as one of the most natural driving talents to come out of off-road racing. His colorful winning ways, good looks and easygoing charm have made him a natural celebrity, popular with both fans and newsmen. Off-roading is still too young to have produced many solid professionals, but Ferro appears destined for more than dune buggy competition alone. He insists, however, that he will continue competing in such events even if he should someday wind up in Victory Lane at Indianapolis—and that could happen. Ferro has already tried road racing in Formula 5000 machinery at Riverside, and made an impressive showing. No one was particularly surprised, either. Least of all Ferro.

"I've wanted to be a race driver since . . .well, about as long as I can remember," he said after winning the Baja 500 in 1971. Ferro drove that race in a single-seat, two-liter VW Sandmaster dune buggy, touring the 558 miles without help in 11 hours and 11 minutes—knocking 44 minutes off the record set a year earlier by Parnelli Jones.

Ferro learned his craft as a rough-and-tumble desert motorcycle racer with District 37 of the American Motorcycle Association while still in high school. After two years with the Army, and decoration for service in Vietnam, Ferro returned to bike racing in 1969 and that year won the Checker motorcycle hare and hounds championship. Then he began to think about buggies.

"I figured that was the best way to get started racing," he said. "You can learn a lot about handling a car and how to treat them, and you don't have such a big investment. It's safer too."

Bobby built a Wampuskitty VW buggy and entered the 1970 Baja 500. He was running second when he rolled it, but finished well just the same—testimony to the nature of the sport and its competitors. In November that same year Bobby took the buggy to Baja for the 1000-miler and, with co-driver Doyle Fields, finished second in class. People were already watching this young man, because it wasn't many weeks later that Don Arnett of Sandmaster hired Bobby to drive the Sandmaster single-seater in all the big off-road events. It was a good business partnership for both parties. Bobby immediately began winning just about every race he entered, including the Baja 500, the Hi Desert 250, Adelanto 200, Snore 250 (after starting in twenty-seventh position) and the Westward Ho 200 in 1971. These overall victories were backed by his single-seat buggy class win in 1971 in the Mexican 1000 (again no help), and second overall in the race just 17 minutes behind Parnelli Jones in the powerful Bronco Colt.

When asked what he thought of Ferro's promise as a race driver,

Jones smiled and said: "I'm sure we'll hear a lot more from him, and soon."

Bobby prefers riding alone because it gives him full responsibility for whatever happens—good or bad.

"I wouldn't want to blow it for somebody else," he said. "And I certainly wouldn't want somebody screwing things up for me either."

Bobby's success isn't just credited to generous driving talent. He works hard at racing, takes it very seriously and always tries to pre-run a course more than once before a race—especially in Baja. His experience with dirt bikes has paid off too. As one observer put it: "Bobby comes across the rock-strewn desert in a buggy as if if were a bike, making trails where there are none, and generally riding the tops of the ruts."

His success is also partly due to the super reliable equipment at his disposal. Engine wizard Scott MacKenzie says that Bobby never had a big engine during his string of unprecedented wins in 1971

Veteran desert racer Dick Hansen of San Diego gets a good luck wish from an admirer before start of 1972 Baja 500. Hansen, usually a top finisher, didn't complete the 558-mile grind this time.

in the sturdy Sandmaster buggy. MacKenzie said he preferred to put a more docile but reliable engine in the buggy. So during the 1971 season Bobby was driving a 1900cc VW mill with a single carburetor. But in June 1972 MacKenzie decided the roads in Baja for the 500 were getting faster and smoother, and that Bobby would need more suds under the hood. Things looked grim, however, when Ferro drew number 293 for a starting position. Leaving that late in the field puts a driver at a disadvantage for several reasons. It means he will have to do more driving in the dark, pass more vehicles, the dirt will be chewed up more and the dust will be worse. But despite all those obstacles, Ferro roared through the field to become the first driver to score back-to-back wins in the 500, and the first to complete the trek in under 11 hours. His time was a sizzling 10 hours and 56 minutes.

But while Ferro may be one of the kings of Baja and other races, Fritz Kroyer, a tall, lanky native of Denmark, has built a similar reputation for his feats in the Nevada desert. Teamed with Bill Harkey, a rugged yet gentle man in his fifties, Kroyer has blitzed the field twice in the Mint 400 to capture top honors as the overall winner among four-wheel vehicles.

Humble and shy, Kroyer is a master mechanic who hates to abuse his machinery and frets constantly that the car is falling apart under the punishment. In 1971, the first year he and Harkey won the Mint race, Kroyer said he was sure the car was about to give up as he started the final lap.

"I knew I had the race won if I could just keep the thing together one more lap," Kroyer said in his slightly accented English. "But I kept hearing all kinds of funny noises that I hadn't noticed before. I was a nervous wreck until I saw the finish line."

But in a move that typifies Kroyer's amazing skill, the twenty-nine-year-old Californian overcame his fears and turned that final round into the fastest lap of the race. He also hates to give up the wheel once he slides into the cockpit. Chewing a giant wad of gum furiously to keep his mouth moist, Fritz drove five hours straight before turning the car over to Harkey for just one lap.

Like Ferro, Fritz takes his driving seriously and has his sights set on a career in racing. Although he admits to an interest in other forms of motoring competition, Kroyer would like to concentrate on the off-road variety and is already well on his way to making a good living at it. Fritz figures that with his winnings from one or two major races a year, which can approach $10,000, and some help from sponsors it would be possible to turn professional. Fritz realizes that physical conditioning is also important, and to keep in shape he jogs a couple of miles every morning and stays away from tobacco. Although his spectacular driving brings cheers from the fans, Kroyer is no grandstander—he aims to please only himself.

"The guy who can win a race at the slowest possible speed, that's what any kind of racing is all about," he said. "Preserve the car at all costs. Why win a race by a margin of two hours, and risk wrecking the car, when you can win it by two minutes?"

Kroyer doesn't view off-road racing as man-against-man competition, but rather man against terrain. Even speed is only one element to winning. "I'll drive fast if I have to. But our buggies aren't designed for really high speeds. When you get up around 80 or 90 miles per hour with them, you're making them do something they weren't designed for and they can be unsafe."

Kroyer is a perfectionist about almost everything. He literally goes over every nut and bolt on the buggy before a race, and if he makes a driving error it both angers and embarrasses him. At a race one year in California's picturesque Borrego Desert east of San Diego, Fritz lost the brakes on his buggy and flipped right at the starting line in front of ninety percent of the spectators.

"There were so many people there watching me that I wanted to just crawl in a hole and hide," he said.

But as much fun as desert racing is for Kroyer, there are some tedious moments. "When I was crashing through those gullies in the Mint, I'd be thinking, 'You stupid idiot, what are you *doing* here?' But that thought passed right away. I knew exactly what I was doing there."

What motivates Fritz?

"Money," is his one-word answer. "You can make a lot of money racing. Most drivers don't, of course. But a few do. I intend to." And his penetrating pale blue eyes radiate the confidence behind those words.

But long before Fritz Kroyer and Bobby Ferro achieved some degree of stardom, a young Volkswagen mechanic in Spring Valley, a suburb of San Diego, was already on his way to a new career—even before he knew it. And he wouldn't have believed it even if a fortune teller had told him.

Johnny Johnson and his pretty wife Linda just wanted to have fun. It was a hobby of sorts. A fun way to pass the evenings, and something to do together on the weekends. Neither dreamed that building the silly sand buggy in the garage would someday make them rich and famous. Well, maybe not rich—just yet, anyway. But certainly famous. It was Johnson, you may remember, who took George Plimpton on that bouncy ride from Ensenada to La Paz while television cameras whirred from nearly every direction to capture the high-speed adventure for a network television special. But Johnson was already established as one of the top buggy drivers on the scene long before Plimpton ever heard of Baja California or off-road racing. Johnson has a string of major victories that is, and may remain, unequaled. In many of those races Linda was at his side reading the map and keeping him posted minute by minute. At the Mint 400 in 1969 Johnny and Linda teamed up in their homemade Corvair buggy to win not only the experimental class, but capture overall honors as the fastest four-wheel vehicle.

Although their performance was impressive, no one was really very surprised. A year earlier Johnny had shown he was both a brilliant car builder and skilled driver when he and Paul Frank Schwab took first place in the modified class for two-wheel-drive buggies in the Mexican 1000. The next year, a few months after the amazing Las Vegas victory with Linda, Johnny and Dave Donnan brought the Corvair buggy home first again in the experimental class in the big 1000-miler, and placed second in the overall standings. In the 1970 running of the same event Johnny and Larry Bright did it with a first place finish in the competitive modified buggy class.

Johnny has won about every major desert race devised, including the Borrego Rough 100 in 1968 and again in 1969. In the 1972 Mexican 1000, driving a single-seat VW Sandmaster, Johnny drove the entire distance from Mexicali to La Paz quickly enough to take first place in the single-seat buggy category. His only serious competition in that race, won by Parnelli, was dashing Bobby Ferro, who flipped his single-seater halfway through the race and damaged it too badly to continue.

Another pioneer of the sport who has since turned a weekend hobby into a lucrative career is the inimitable Drino Miller of Costa Mesa, California, who has overall honors in both the Mexican 1000 and Mint 400 in Las Vegas.

Miller first became interested in sand buggies while working on a master's degree in political science at UCLA. At that time he had his sights set on a teaching career, but he never quite got around to it. Before he knew it Drino was too busy building buggies and winning races to have time for teaching. Considered one of the more innovative off-roaders, Miller is credited with building the first single-seat buggy for competition and, along with partner Sam Havens, is known as the father of the Baja Bug—now one of the most popular classes in competition. Their mail order and over-the-counter business now offers about every device needed to prepare a VW-based vehicle of any kind for fun or competition.

"I never really thought about buggies and racing as a career," the tall, husky Californian said. "But things just started happening the right way. We got started at the right time."

But if Miller is well endowed with engineering savvy, he hasn't been short-changed in driving talent either. In the 1968 Mexican 1000 Drino teamed with Steve Rieman and placed second in class behind Johnny Johnson. The following year, in the inaugural Baja 500, Drino and Vic Wilson shared driving chores in the single-seater and maneuvered the tricky and treacherous course fast enough to claim a class victory and second overall in the standings. That was the beginning of a brief but brilliant partnership. In 1970, sharing turns at the wheel of the Volkswagen-powered single-seater, Miller and Wilson won not only their class, but overall honors for fastest time in both the Mexican 1000 and Mint 400.

Each year Miller adds to his list of successes, either with class victories or all-out wins, such as at the inaugural Dam 500 in 1971. But winning isn't always everything in this madcap sport. For some, like municipal Court Judge Thomas Duffy, just taking part in the action is rewarding—especially if you can stop along the way and help a colleague.

Duffy, who enters off-road races regularly in his Toyota Land Cruiser, has become known as the Good Samaritan of Baja California. The judge and his sidekick Ken Younghusband, an engineer, earned their honorary title because they frequently stop along the route to help competitors who have broken down or somehow been sidelined.

"We always carry along towing equipment and first-aid stuff," the judge explained. "I'm just not competitive enough to pass up somebody who needs help. As long as we reach the finish before the deadline, I'm happy."

Most racers who receive assistance from Duffy and Younghusband are plenty grateful, but sometimes it backfires. One year during a Baja race the judge and Younghusband stopped to help a factory team whose small Swedish sedan had become mired along the beach route. Duffy and Younghusband hitched up their tow chain and pulled the car free, only to find themselves stuck in the soggy sand. But the team they had helped only waved a thanks and roared off into the night.

Duffy dismisses such things with a gentle shrug, however. "I didn't think much of their attitude," the judge said smiling. "But they're professionals and really wanted to do well."

Duffy and Younghusband did manage to free themselves, and finished the distance under the deadline.

Motorcycles are less in the spotlight in Baja than in the Mint race where they have their own event. But the two-wheel riders can't be ignored, either for their skill or hardy spirit and daring. Among the top two-wheel competitors, although there are dozens of talented and hard riding members of that group, are J. N. Roberts, Gunnar Lindstrom, Max Switzer, Mike Patrick, Phil Bowers,

Malcolm Smith, Larry Berquist and Gary Preston, to mention only a few.

Patrick and Bowers, intense and dedicated to winning, typify their clan. Riding a Yamaha 360, the two young Californians have won the Mint race in Las Vegas, a place they affectionately call their lucky city. But luck has little to do with team's successes. Their idea of luck is spelled p-r-e-p-a-r-a-t-i-o-n.

"There are a lot of great riders up here," Bowers, a school teacher from Chino, said one year before the Mint race. "If we have any edge it's in preparation. Nothing can be left to chance, no matter how trivial it may seem at the time."

Patrick owns a motorcycle shop in Corona, which he purchased with his share of the money the team earned by winning the Mint race two years in a row—1969 and 1970.

Before either Patrick or Bowers fire up the engine they go over their motorcycle as carefully as if it were an Apollo moon project. The engine is torn down completely and each piece is inspected,

Danny (left) and Mickey Thompson are regulars on the off-road circuit. Danny, twenty-two, rides shotgun with his father and also spends 14 to 16 hours a day working on the cars when he isn't racing. Mickey said he hopes the hard work will discourage his son from turning professional race driver, but so far the plan isn't working.

tested and X-rayed to insure against failure out in the Nevada wilderness.

"Odds are the thing Las Vegas is built on," said Patrick. "And we like to reduce the odds by making sure everything is working, and will keep working, on the Yamaha."

It's the same story with Larry Berquist and Gary Preston, who took overall honors in the 1968 Mexican 1000. Both seasoned desert racers, they have become among the most celebrated riders in this country. Yet, like Patrick and Bowers, there is little in their private lives to suggest what they are capable of when they straddle a motorcycle for a weekend of competition. Berquist is a photo-engraver and has been for more than twenty years. He acquired his first motorcycle when he was only twelve years old and began desert racing two years later. For competition, the desert is Larry's first choice. The "other stuff" he considers "boring" by comparison. Preston is proprietor of Gary's Cycle World in Azusa, California, but it's not what you're thinking. The "cycles" Preston sells have pedals. That's right. Bicycles!

Competing together over the years in desert races throughout Southern California, Berquist and Preston became close friends and members of the same motorcycle club. But they never competed as teammates until the inaugural Mexican 1000 in 1967. Berquist, riding a Honda, started the race and led most of the action for the first 275 miles, until a battery shorted out and left him stranded in the Baja desert. Meanwhile, about 150 miles down the road, an anxious Gary Preston waited for a motorcycle and teammate who would never arrive. Things were different the following year, however, and the team held it together for the win.

The men and women mentioned in this chapter are only a small portion of the enthusiastic and hardworking devotees of this sport. But they do serve to demonstrate the growing number of followers and show the broad cross-section of people who help make off-road racing perhaps the most socially and economically integrated sport in the world. No one was deliberately excluded, and many names that have not appeared so far will be mentioned in later chapters.

4 BACKYARD SPECIALS

---→

It started a long time ago over a beer. At first it was just talk mixed with wishing, but in April 1970 the service manager of Wolff Volkswagen in San Diego picked up a 1964 VW chassis. Soon front axle parts and a pair of complete Porsche front brake assemblies, including spindles, were stored in the Wolff workshop. That was enough—the wishing turned to action and four German-born mechanics built a car to compete in the Mexican 1000.

Ernst Schneidereit and Gottfried Ohrdorf, both Wolff employees, assembled the front axle beam with relocated springleaves; relocated stops were fitted with Porsche knuckles. Steel spacers were inserted between the axle beam and the torsion arms. The pair fashioned the tie rods out of pretensioned spring steel for flexibility.

All of the welding on the chassis was done at Wolff's, with every weld doubled for greater strength. The front axle reinforcements were attached to the top and bottom of both sides of the axle beam. The supports extended about two feet under the chassis. The shock absorber was a carbon-type "two-striper" Bilstein gas shock. The steering damper was standard VW.

"The brake hose from the support to the wheel was later covered with material that could not be easily penetrated by gravel," explained Dieter Plambeck, a salesman who acts as spokesman for the German foursome of Schneidereit, Ohrdorf, Karl DieKamp and himself.

"We chose a solid mount on the front of the transmission and a cage with the rear mounts made of partially depressed rubber mounts, allowing a certain amount of flexibility," Plambeck said.

"It did not involve any great problem. However, there were differences of opinion among the group as to the durability, road-

One of the more successful forerunners of the now popular Baja Bug class was the Baja Wolff, prepared by two German-born mechanics, Ernst Schneidereit and Gottfried Ohrdorf, in San Diego. The car is basically stock except for beefed-up suspension and some engine modifications like a Crower V-12 camshaft and highlift rocker arms and stronger valve springs.

ability and flexibility of the mounts under extreme conditions.

"We found it necessary to reinforce and modify the rear shock absorber brackets and install dual Bilstein gas pressure shocks—four-stripers—since we knew the vehicle was going to be quite heavy," Plambeck added.

A trial run of the bug in September 1970 proved that single-shock suspension was adequate and one shock absorber on each side of the car was removed. Also as a result of the test run, the differential was modified to accommodate four pinion gears, and third and fourth gears were reduced to 1.48 and 1.14 to compensate for bigger tires.

The engine, a 1970 Beetle vintage, was completely balanced and blueprinted. The 1600cc powerplant was fitted with a Crower V-12 camshaft of 240 degrees duration. Highlift rocker arms and stronger valve springs were used. In order to get a better filling into the cylinders, Ohrdorf installed dual intake heads and a dual intake manifold. A Zenith 32ND11X carburetor and a centrifugal distributor, which is sealed internally against dust, along with an external oil cooler and an exhaust header system mark the extent of modifications on the engine.

"We found it necessary to install an in-line fuel filter to prevent dirt from the gas tanks entering and possibly blocking the carburetor," Plambeck said.

After the installation of engine and transmission, the car was equipped with 15-inch Tacoma wheels, with a five-inch offset in the front and an eight-inch offset in the rear. The front tires were Semperit radials, tube-type with "dog bone" pattern, while 900 x 15 Firestone flotation tires were used on the rear wheels.

The team entered the bug in the Mexican 1000 less than a month after it was finished. The rugged grind was not only the maiden voyage for the Baja Wolff, it was the first race for either Schneidereit or Ohrdorf. They finished twenty-second overall and third in class with a time of 21 hours flat.

"Actually, we could have knocked at least an hour and a half off our elapsed time," Dieter said. "But we took it too easy. It was the first race for Ernst and Gottfried and they weren't sure how the car would hold up."

A broken bolt on the rear shock absorber cost them a few minutes of precious time near El Arco, and a malfunction in the gas gauge kept the team in the dark about fuel consumption. But otherwise it was a smooth trip—at least for Baja.

Incidentally when the car became movable and was pushed out of the Wolff shop for its christening celebration, Plambeck couldn't find a bottle of champagne. So the Baja Wolff was baptized—like the dream—with a bottle of beer.

Putting together an off-road racing machine requires more imagination and ingenuity than money. Because of that probably about ninety percent of the cars used are made or modified by amateur car builders in somebody's garage during the evening hours and weekends. Modifying a stock Volkswagen Beetle is rapidly becoming one of the more popular avenues to off-road competition for obvious reasons—it requires less labor and skill, and certainly less money. Numerous Baja Bug clubs are springing up everywhere, and they hold events of their own, usually exclusively for modified bugs. NORRA even established a class especially for the little rigs in 1971, and it is already one of the largest classes going.

But if competing in a VW sedan, however modified, isn't exactly what you had in mind, don't worry. Building a dune buggy is only slightly more expensive and not much more work. That is, of course, assuming you are one of those handy types who can read instructions and use a little imagination, or "Mexineering" as off-road folks like to call it.

No one knows for sure just how many dune buggies have been built to date, but a conservative estimate would be somewhere in the neighborhood of 40,000 to 50,000. But the figure could easily go twice that high. Most of these are done with the aid of a car kit. The kit cars, like the Meyers Manx or EMPI Imp to mention only two of dozens, are designed to be put together by anybody. They require very little in the way of tools or technical skill. All you have to do is follow the step-by-step instructions supplied by the manufacturers and, in as little as 40 hours (some do it in less time), you can be ready for a test ride. The cost generally runs from about $500 and up, depending on initial cost of the kit, Volkswagen parts and where you buy them, and just how fancy you want the buggy.

There are those among us who would prefer not to get our hands dirty, don't have the time or just plain don't have the manual and mental skills necessary. No problem if you have a little extra bread. Just contract with anyone of several car builders (most of them, however, are in the Los Angeles and San Diego areas) who are in the business for just that reason. They can usually turn out a buggy within a few days (depending on how many orders they have at the moment) for under $2000. A racing machine, however, can cost several times that amount. Unfortunately, perhaps, there are rarely bargains in this business and any "cut-rate" deals should be investigated—or avoided. That's not to say it doesn't pay to shop around, either for quality or price, but just don't expect any super deals. Although most buggy manufacturers are both respectable and reliable, there are, sadly, a few who are not. This doesn't imply that a small operation, and there are many of those, is either crooked or shady. Many of these small shops turn out high quality equipment. But it would be wise to check with either experienced hobbyists or satisfied customers before investing any money.

There are a few "bootleg" operations around that stay in business only long enough to make a few bucks. What they usually do is buy one of the established fiberglass bodies, pull a quick mold off it and start selling copies. In most of these the quality is pretty shabby. The bodies are roughly finished, don't fit very well and the glass is apt to be rather thin in places. Sometimes these defects or poor workmanship can be spotted before buying, but more often than not the customer doesn't learn the truth until he begins assemblying his buggy at home. Then, of course, it's too late.

Another thing to consider is which model to buy—deluxe or economy. The deluxe kits usually contain everything you will need to build the buggy, short of the necessary VW parts. Most manufacturers offer cheaper kits that contain basic fiberglass parts, but no hardware, windshield or other refinements. You may not need these, or already have them. But if not, buying them later could end up costing you more than the price of a deluxe kit to begin with. This should be carefully considered before buying.

Now, assuming you have decided on the right body kit, the next step is locating the engine, frame and running gear. Again careful shopping and planning are imperative. Most builders agree that the 1961 and later VW engines and transmissions are the best bet. Earlier models had the 36-horsepower engine and a non-synchro low gear transaxle. It's just too primitive and gutless for today's needs. The 40-horsepower engine came out in 1961, along with the all-synchro transmission. Even though there have been several engine changes since then, the newer parts will interchange with the 40-horsepower engine if you should want to make any modifications for more power. But almost nothing from 1961 and later will interchange with the 36-horsepower mills. However, there is nothing wrong with pre-1961 frames and front ends, so if you can find one of these in good shape, don't hesitate. Don't bother buying a Karmann Ghia, however. There aren't any buggy kits that fit its wider chassis. Stick with the little bug and everything will size up just right, assuming you bought a good fiberglass body. It's generally a relatively simple bolt-on project that requires more time and effort than engineering skill.

Finding a wrecked VW shouldn't be difficult and need not be expensive. Your best bet is one that has been bent up enough to make it too costly to repair, but the damage should be confined primarily to the body work. Make sure the frame, engine and running gear are still sound. Rollovers are usually the best bet. Check the aforementioned parts carefully. Prices vary considerably from town to town and in various parts of the country. The dune buggy craze has sent the value of wrecked VW parts soaring in the past three or four years, particularly in places like Southern California. It depends entirely on how strong the buggy-building action is, but sometimes it may be worth while to drive a considerable distance if the savings warrant the trip.

You can buy all the parts individually, but it may be simpler and cheaper to buy the whole car if you locate one that fills your

Schneidereit and Ohrdorf used an aluminum skid plate in the rear to protect engine, exhaust header system and rear axle from gravel and rocks. A similar plate was installed in front (below) as protection for front axle.

needs. If you choose that route, then your first step is to begin disassembling the car to salvage what you need for a buggy. About the only thing you will need in the way of special equipment for this job is metric tools and a cutting torch. In most places these items can be rented. If not, try borrowing them from trusting friends. If you have to farm the work out or buy tools it will add to the cost of building the buggy.

Once you are ready, the best place to start is by removing the seats and the helper springs used for adjustment. Next take out the battery, hold-down strap and cover. The gas tank should come out next. Be sure to plug the line before removing it if it contains fuel, and save the four rectangular hold-down washers.

The steering column is next to go, and can be taken out by removing the clamping bolt at the bottom end of the shaft. Then remove the two bolts and clamp at the upper end of the column and save them. Also be sure to save the rubber strip at the upper end and the rubber grommet at the lower end of the column for future use.

One of the most tedious jobs is removing the wiring harness. As you do this, be sure to tag all disconnected ends for future reference. Otherwise you may be lost in a maze of confusion and frustration. It would also be a good idea to check the VW owner's service manual which contains a color-coded diagram of the wiring. It's almost a must for everyone except the most expert auto electricians and VW mechanics. If the wiring appears worn and ragged, special buggy wiring harnesses are available from several buggy builders and some VW dealers. If you have any doubts, spring for the new wiring. Electrical problems can be some of the most troublesome and time-consuming automotive woes. The gamble is rarely worth it, especially since you already have started taking things apart.

Next it is best to remove the following: speedometer and drive cable, ignition switch with bolt, light switch, gas gauge and sending cable, windshield wiper and switch, horn, tail lights, license plate light, turn indicator lights, fuse block, rear view mirror, brake reservoir and front floor mats. Be sure to keep all of the nuts and bolts or other attaching parts that go with these components.

Now that you've pretty well stripped the body, the next step is to remove it from the frame. This is another relatively simple job of unfastening bolts, unless they are frozen with rust. Occasionally some cutting and/or drilling is necessary, but you may be lucky. The attaching bolts are located under the back seat, rear fenders, running boards and gas tank. Save the rectangular washers from under the running boards. Now the body can be lifted off the frame and forgotten.

Since most buggies (especially for competition) are two-seaters, you will have to shorten the chassis. (This isn't necessary, however, if you purchase one of the big four-seat kits.) If you don't intend to do this job yourself look around for a shop that is experienced in this sort of operation. It isn't difficult, but if it gets fouled up you'll be right back where you started—looking for another wrecked VW. Having the frame cut usually costs from $75 to $100. If anybody wants more than that, better look around some more. If they are charging less, you have found either a real bargain or someone who doesn't know what he's doing.

Removing the suspension, transaxle or engine isn't necessary, but it makes the cutting job easier. It is necessary, however, to remove all the sound-deadening material from the rear floor pan to just forward of the brake pedal. This can be done with a putty knife. Disconnect the main brake line from the "T" fitting at the rear so it can be bent forward out of the way of the area where the cut is to be made. Also remove the access covers at the front of the floor pan and at the rear. Disconnect the coupler between the gearshift linkage and the transaxle, and leave the coupler on the transaxle. This should be done through the rear access hole. Next step is to remove the gear shift lever assembly, carefully noting the position of the shift plate under the cover. This guide plate serves to incorporate the reverse lock-out, which is on the passenger side of the car pointing upward. The gear lever linkage tube can be removed through the front access cover.

The emergency brake cables and the emergency brake lever should also be taken off. As should the pedal assembly, throttle wire and clutch cable, the battery holder and ground strap. Also take off the heater control wire and replace the handle. It will now be necessary to enlarge the rear access hole to simplify the cutting operation. This can be done by putting the access cover in place and scribing a line around it on the surface of the tunnel top. Then remove the access cover and measure in one-half inch and scribe a new line parallel to the outside line or outside edge of where the cover had been, leaving enough metal to keep clutch and throttle wire tubes secure. Enlarge the hole by cutting along the inside line.

The next step is to mark the lines for the chassis cut. Most kits require removal of about a 14½-inch section of chassis. Some kits differ, however. The correct measurement will be included in the instructions. First scribe a line even with the rear ends of the seat tracks straight across the floor. Then measure backward the specified distance and draw another line parallel to the first one. Now you are ready (although perhaps a little edgy) to start cutting. Be careful when cutting across the tunnel top not to cut through any of the various tubes that are in there. With the tunnel top removed you will be able to get to these tubes. The two tubes nearest the top lead to the emergency brake opening. It may be necessary to braze these short tubes back onto the bracket just under the emergency brake opening. Reach through the enlarged rear access hole with the torch and cut the emergency brake tubes near the torsion bar housing. The heater cable tubes can be cut in both front and rear since they won't be used. Just inside the rear access hole, the throttle, clutch and, on early models, the choke guide tubes pass through the driver's side, where they are welded to the floor pan. Using the torch, cut through the weld and the tubes, leaving them unfastened. Now finish cutting out the section to be removed and dress up the rough edges with a disc grinder.

Fitting the two halves together requires taking measurements to be certain that length and side-to-side wheelbase are correct. While moving the two halves together, the loosened guide tubes must be pulled through and out the rear of the floor pan. These will be longer than necessary and can be shortened later. The clutch tube is the only one with a critical length, since it must be cut precisely to accommodate the flexible clutch cable guide tube that is positioned just above the transaxle front cover.

Now you are ready to start welding, and the way to begin is with a series of tack welds not more than six inches apart, alternating from one side of the floor pan to the other. Leave eight inches unwelded at the outer edges so that necessary darts can be cut from the rear part of the pan. The kit will include a template for cutting these darts. Just make sure that everything lines up before starting to weld, otherwise you won't get the body to fit right. Even if it did fit you would soon have one hell of a lot of other headaches with everything from tires to running gear. So be meticulous about this part. The next step is to weld in between the tack welds. Be sure to turn the pan over and weld the bottom of the tunnel area.

Braze the throttle, clutch and choke tubes back into place just inside the rear access hole. The clutch tube should be hacksawed off approximately 1¾ inches behind the floor pan. Next install the flexible clutch cable guide tube between the guide tube on the floor pan and the boss cast into the front transaxle cover. The flexible tube should be pre-loaded to sag approximately one inch for proper clutch operation.

Clutch, throttle, choke and emergency brake cables and wires can be shortened either by looping them and securing with clamps, or by cutting them to length and swaging new ends on with a kit. The main brake line should be inserted through the hole in the rear of the floor pan and pulled through back to the "T" fitting. Make sure that it doesn't kink and is secured. The gear shift assembly linkage must be shortened the same amount as was removed from the chassis before it is put back into place. Mark the tube so the straight section at the rear can be removed. Scribe a line on the tube parallel to its axis to eliminate any chance of the two halves rotating after the cut has been made. After installation don't forget to safety wire the setscrew in the coupler. The two bolts on top of the tunnel are part of the shift level adjustment. By loosening and sliding the cover plate forward or backward and tightening again, you can control the top or bottom of the shift pattern.

At this point it may be necessary to reshape the tunnel with a five-pound hammer to allow the seat frame to clear in its rearmost position.

After these modifications the chassis can be cleaned and painted. Then bleed the brakes and check the level of the oil in the steering box. The rubber mounting strip from the VW should be glued around the perimeter of the chassis and the shock mounting bolts turned around so they can be removed to change shocks when the fiberglass buggy body is mounted.

Before mounting the body it is advisable to give the underside a generous coating of underseal, both to protect it and to cut down on road noise. It is also a good idea to perform a little finish sanding, too, since most bodies are often somewhat rough. This can, of course, be handled after installation if you're getting anxious to put the whole package together.

The hard part is—or should be—over now. Installing the fiberglass body is a fairly simple job for anyone who has gotten this far with the project. There will be satisfactory instructions in the kit to preclude giving a bolt-by-bolt description here, but it might be worthwhile to offer a couple of hints: Don't expect the body to fit perfectly. That just isn't the nature of fiberglass. It probably will be necessary to do a little wedging and clamping to get it in place, and by all means do the fitting and clamping before drilling the mounting holes.

Once everything is assembled it will be important to check several things, including toe-in, caster angle and rear wheel camber. The buggy body is considerably lighter than the metal sedan structure, so these suspension elements will probably have to be adjusted.

The only thing left now will be selecting wheels and tires, but this does require close attention. Thanks to the growing popularity of dune buggies and off-road racing, there are several brands of tires now on the market designed to fit just about every need and situation. Shop around and explain your particular needs. If there are any buggy enthusiasts or clubs in the area, check with them. Most buggy drivers now are using wheels with seven-inch rims in

Dust is always a major problem in off-road events, so the two mechanics installed this air filter system with a fan to pressurize the passenger compartment and keep dust out.

front and 10-inch rims in the rear. Again the main criteria for choosing the best wheels depend mostly on how and where the buggy will be used—don't be too hasty in making a decision.

As the preceding indicates, building a street or sand buggy can be a relatively easy and inexpensive project. But preparing a machine for racing is another story. It's basically the same job, but the refinements to engine and suspension make a big difference. Another major consideration is safety. Both NORRA and IDRA, as well as most responsible clubs around, have stringent safety regulations for cars. Generally they are the same, or very similar. Roll cages and safety belts and harnesses are the obvious requirements, but there are often small details that can be described in competition rules from the clubs or organizations and would be too involved for us here.

Most race drivers, especially the better ones, have lots of secrets and they aren't too willing to share them. But since durability is one of the major ingredients for success in off-road racing, quality workmanship is probably as important as imaginative engineering. Maybe more so.

Many top drivers still rely on *basically* stock equipment, although that still leaves a wide margin for interpretation. A good running engine might get you by, but it will almost certainly be necessary to beef up the suspension. Heavier shocks, torsion bars and possibly a limiting strap to keep wheel travel from increasing over the rough terrain are almost essential. Instrumentation in the VW is pretty skimpy (usually only a speedometer and a fuel gauge), so it might be a good idea to invest in at least oil pressure and electrical charge indicators.

Another essential for safer racing is an air horn. Visibility in off-road racing, even in daylight, is often limited to a few yards. If you are approaching another vehicle the driver may not see you coming, or may not be *able* to see you, and a quick blast of the horn can save you both a lot of trouble and anxiety.

Seat comfort is obviously very important in something as rough and bouncy as off-road racing. Some drivers still get by using stock VW seats, but not many. Invest in a contoured fiberglass bucket job and glue a slab of foam rubber onto it. It won't necessarily look pretty, but you'll be thankful after the first mile or so. These seats really keep the driver and passenger firmly in place, and it is amazing how much you can get jostled around when you're bouncing across the desert even at only 30 or 40 mph. It doesn't take long for your posterior to protest. If you aren't comfortable at the wheel you tend to fight yourself. There's more than enough to fight in an off-road event without having to add your own body to the list.

In most buggies there will be a small storage area immediately behind the seats. This can be used to carry a few tools, plus some spare parts like spark plugs, points, condenser and various other odds and ends that might need replacing in the middle of nowhere. And don't forget also to save room for a few sandwiches, some cookies and a bottle or two of Gatorade.

It is also advisable to take along such items as plugs and patches for tires, a CO_2 bottle for inflating tires, some wire, heavy duty tape, liquid silicone, motor oil and heavy jackets—just in case you get stranded even after all this preparation. It still happens to more than half the entries in every race. Keep those odds in mind and it will be easier to remember what to take along.

There are a lot of goodies on the market to give the VW engine more zing. Whether to opt for added horsepower at the possible expense of reliability is up to you. Many of the most successful drivers like Andy DeVercelly, Drino Miller, Fritz Kroyer and Bob Ferro are very conservative when it comes to adding power. They prefer adding strength wherever possible. One place it pays to add a little armor is under the engine and transmission. Some ⅞-inch aluminum plating will do the job nicely. It adds minimal weight, but can prevent a lot of damage.

Not everyone follows the line of thinking that mild engines and reliability are synonymous. Johnny Johnson has some different ideas on that subject. In fact a lot of his ideas about building buggies are pretty unorthodox. Even by off-road standards!

Take the wheelbase for example. Everyone knows that the stock wheelbase of a Volkswagen (94.5 inches) is too long. It adds to the chance of bottoming out at the tops of steep ridges. So, as described earlier, most buggy bodies are designed to fit an 80-inch frame— requiring the builder to cut 14½ inches out of the chassis. But when Johnny was putting together his machine he thought about two things that most people forget. One is that a short wheelbase does absolutely nothing for the handling of a car at high speed and, second, that there are very few steep ridges on the major race courses. So Johnny built a full 100 inches between the front wheels and those in back when he put together one of the first buggies with a tubular frame.

That was just the first of many departures from tradition for the former mechanic. Another rule in race car building is to keep the center of gravity as low as possible for better cornering. Most off-road vehicles are much higher in that regard than other varieties, but few match the profile of Johnny's buggy which is more than five

That powder-fine dust can also ruin the inside of an engine in a few minutes if it filters through the carburetor, so Schneidereit and Ohrdorf installed this sealed air duct running through the passenger compartment with an air intake on the roof. Filter is located inside the passenger compartment where air is relatively dust free.

feet from the ground to the top of the roll cage. Part of this is to give the car a ground clearance of 14 inches and the rest is for driver comfort. Johnson wanted the roll cage high enough to prevent rapping his head while bouncing along, or in case of a flip. To achieve this margin of safety he built the cage so it stands eight inches higher than his head.

Weight is always a subject of concern for race car builders. But again Johnson ignored tradition. Starting with heavier frame components for more durability, Johnson ended up with a buggy that weighed in at more than 1600 pounds—nearly as much as a stock VW sedan. He even went so far as to use a 30-gallon gas tank that weighs 186 pounds when full.

"The added weight really doesn't hurt the handling that much in off-road racing," he said. "I think a heavier, more solid machine will take the bumps better and hold up longer. Anyway I'd rather have the strength and added safety over the performance you might gain by cutting weight."

A simple philosophy that works well. At least for Johnson. But then he could afford the few extra pounds his winning buggy carried, because there was more horsepower pushing it. Instead of the VW engine, Johnny opted for the more powerful, but heavier, Corvair air-cooled six-cylinder powerplant.

When Johnson and his wife Linda first showed up at off-road races with the Corvair-powered rig, there were more than a few skeptics in the pits. These fascinating Detroit-made mills had been tried before, rarely with much success. But Johnson was using an engine built by Ted Trevor, who has a way with such things. Johnny was never very talkative about what was used inside the engine, and during an interview with magazine writer Ed Orr, the conversation went something like this:

Orr: "What have you got in it?"

Johnson: "Lots of things."

Orr: "A cam?"

Johnson: "Yeah."

Orr: "What kind?"

Johnson: "Hot."

Orr: "What's the bore?"

Johnson: "Large."

Orr: "Stroke?"

Pictures show shop of
Chenowth Racing Products
in Spring Valley, California,
builder of dune buggies
and accessories. Dozens of
such operations are springing up throughout Southern
California. Owner Lynn
Chenowth started out mak-
ing drag racing cars and accessories, now has switched
almost exclusively to off-
road equipment.

Drilling screw holes for exhaust flanges for VW and
Corvair engines.

Welding brackets for special dune buggy fuel tanks.

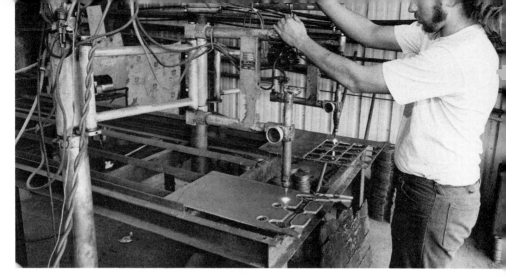

Using automatic gas torch to cut out and shape exhaust flanges.

Above: Building a tubular single-seat buggy frame.

This is the new five-speed Hewland gearbox usually seen in Can-Am Group 7 racers such as the McLarens. Notice inboard brakes for added strength. Indicates how sophisticated buggy building is becoming.

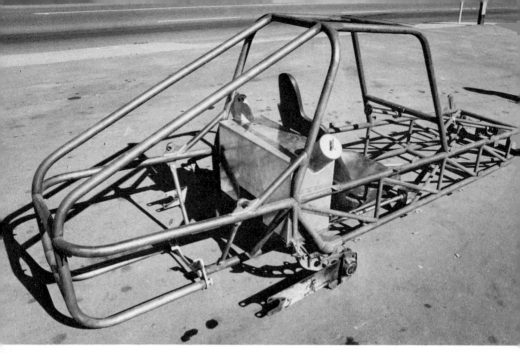

Chenowth sells these lightweight tubular buggy frames in both single-
and double-seat models. Purchaser can add his own engine, suspension
and running gear.

Optional equipment includes this adjustable clutch and brake assembly.

Johnson: "Not stock."

So it goes. Not everyone can afford to have a master engine builder perform magic on his machinery, but Johnson has proved in just about every major off-road race that a hot engine can hold up if it is put together right. As off-road racing inevitably grows more competitive each year, more drivers are forced to gamble with goodies that squeeze a few extra ounces of power out of their engines. Unfortunately for the amateur, engine building can be both expensive and tricky for other than at least a competent mechanic.

Johnson's unconventional approach to buggy building didn't end there, however. To squeeze even more power out of the Corvair he set up a turbocharger outfit—an item that isn't easy to hide. Johnson claimed the turbocharger boosted the power about 20 to 30 percent, but it failed on him one year about halfway through the Baja 500 and ruined his chances of a class win. Even with the power loss, however, he finished in the money as usual. With the whole operation working right, Johnson said his buggy could clip along at 140 mph on fairly decent roads (?) in a race like the Mexican 1000.

The front end assembly is Volkswagen, but not entirely in factory stock condition. Johnson cut the torsion tubes on both sides of the center set screw and rotated the piece before rewelding. This was done to increase the ground clearance. It also increased the trailing arm effect so that the first two inches of travel are toward the rear rather than upward. To gain more wheel travel on the front he cut off the stops between the trailing arms. Johnson also installed a quick-steering conversion kit and super spring steel tie rods that have now all but eliminated the bent tie rod problem that sidelined many buggy racers in the early days. These rods are pre-bent in a slight curve so that when the car hits a really big bump the rods give and then snap back into their original position.

Success in motor racing of any kind demands that you be both thorough and inventive. Johnson exemplifies this as much as anyone in off-road racing, and more than most. In addition to being imaginative and almost flamboyant in overall design, Johnson is a

Lynn Chenowth (left) shows off-road champion Johnny Johnson how easily new cylindrical fuel tank fits into any buggy.

stickler for detail—such as welding the bottom bracket of the steering box to the torsion tubes. This keeps the unit from rotating or sliding sideways should the bolts come loose. Yet it still makes for easy and quick changing of the unit if it breaks. And in case that should happen, Johnson is prepared with an extra unit which he always takes along for insurance.

Good brakes are always important in racing, and Johnson didn't overlook this angle. Front brakes on a buggy don't do much work because of the light weight of the front end. For this reason he elected to stick with the stock VW equipment. The rear end is a different story. Since the rear shoes carry the biggest load, Johnny decided on 2½-inch-wide, self-adjusting Corvair parts. He said the combination gave him the added stopping power and reliability he needed and could depend on.

Buggy technology seems primitive alongside most other forms of motor racing. That is part of its widespread appeal. Despite such exotic rigs as the Bronco Colt and Baja Boot, the simple VW sedan and its hybrid cousin the dune buggy remain the most popular choice of off-roaders. Johnny Johnson and his buggy and the gang at Wolff Motors illustrate the kind of backyard engineering that has made the sport so popular. While money is always an asset, it in no way insures success. Nor does its absence promise only failure and frustration. A limited budget can foster a great deal of creative thinking. The old saw about necessity being the mother of invention was never more true than in off-roading. There are literally hundreds of amateur buggy builders and hobbyists around the country who each day discover new methods of squeezing extra performance and reliability out of a basically simple and economical racing machine. Regulations imposed by sponsoring clubs and organizations generally serve as purely safety measures and rarely inhibit new ideas for better equipment.

The value of experience is priceless. Most drivers, including Johnson, say their best ideas grew out of lessons they learned on the road—the final examination.

5 THE GRANDDADDY OF THEM ALL: A HISTORY OF THE MEXICAN 1000

Those folks who think off-road racing is primitive now should have been around in the beginning. Sure it's still rough and challenging, but there was a time when . . .

Baja California has always stood as something of a Last Frontier to the more adventurous-minded living north of the border. Once affluent *americanos* discovered they really could drive the distance from Tijuana, just across the border from San Diego, to La Paz, near the southern tip of the peninsula, it was normal evolution that someone had to see how fast the trip could be made. La Paz. It means "The Peace" in Spanish. But you go through hell to arrive there. That was the idea. The challenge. Long before there was such a thing as a Mexican 1000 several hardy souls were already addicted to the idea of setting speed records down the peninsula.

Most of their efforts won little public attention. But that didn't dim their enthusiasm even a little. What the hell did it matter anyway if no one knew? Satisfaction was what mattered. Personal satisfaction. Most of those who tried it didn't make much of a dent in history. Mostly because they didn't make it to La Paz. Or, if they did complete the distance, their time wouldn't exactly impress anybody. But there were some . . .

Motorcyclist Dave Ekins set the first known cross-country speed record down Baja. In March 1962 he rode a 250cc Honda Scrambler from Tijuana to La Paz in 39 hours and 56 minutes. Just how fast Ekins had really traveled became startlingly evident a few weeks later when Bill Stroppe led a fleet of Chevrolet trucks on an endurance run from Tijuana to La Paz. Driving at a "normal" pace without trying to set any speed records, Stroppe and his followers took ten days for the trip. This particular expedition was widely publicized by Chevrolet as "The Roughest Run Under the Sun," and became the theme of the firm's truck advertising later that year.

National attention had now been drawn to Baja. Interest picked up considerably. There were dozens of reported efforts during the following four years to better Ekins' speed mark, but all of them failed—either because they never made it, or were too slow.

Then in May 1966 Dave and his brother, Bud Ekins, teamed with dirt track star Eddie Mulder in a barely successful assault on the original mark. The bikes this time were 650cc Triumph TR-6s and the time was 39 hours and 48 minutes—an improvement of only eight minutes. Cliff Coleman also joined in the run, but he didn't reach La Paz until nearly five hours later.

Word was spreading now. Two-wheelers were conquering the peninsula. The idea of staying on a bike over that kind of terrain for nearly a thousand miles was frightening, incredible, almost impossible. Yes, *almost* impossible. That was the attraction—even to make the distance was a real accomplishment. But to do it faster, *better*, was like achieving nirvana. And, of course, more would come.

In June 1966 Al Baker Jr. and his fifteen-year-old son, Al

Baker III, rode a pair of Hodaka 90s from Tijuana to La Paz in 60 hours, setting a record for motorcycles of under 100cc displacement. A figure for still smaller motorcycles, those under 50cc, was established in February 1967 by John Klocker on a Hercules, with a time of 70 hours 30 minutes. Bill Blakeslee tried to follow on another Hercules, but had to quit for repairs at El Arco.

So the motorcyclists had paved another frontier. But could four-wheel vehicles follow? Sure they could make the distance, but could they ever hope to get there quickly enough to brag about it? Four-wheel-drive vehicles were obviously equipped for the trip, but they were slow compared to the lightweight and nimble motorcycles. Or were they?

In January 1967 John Crean and the late John Cummings set the first Baja record for four-wheel vehicles of any kind when they traveled from Tijuana to La Paz in a Meyers Manx buggy in only 29 hours and 17 minutes. But there was a catch. The duo didn't make the trip nonstop, which gave some bide riders the urge to snicker. But they knew better. If a buggy could make the trip in that short a time, someone would come along sooner or later and drive the distance nonstop. Someone. Who? Motoring journals began writing about the conquest of Baja. Buggy enthusiasts didn't have a sport yet, only a weekend hobby. Mental wheels started turning. Somewhere out in the maze of suburbia a buggy was being built, people were plotting. But when would it happen?

All of the attempts so far had followed the same basic route. From Tijuana they drove south through Ensenada and El Rosario, on to Rancho Santa Ynez, Punta Prieta, El Arco and into San Ignacio. From there they headed east through Santa Rosalía and down the Gulf coast through Mulegé. Beyond Bahía Concepción, they turned toward the west through the Comondús and past Pozo Grande. Then they headed south again through Villa Constitucíon and into La Paz. That was the route shown on the map as Highway One. It was *the* road. In total distance it covered 950 miles and, in 1967, included 130 miles of pavement. About half of that was south from Tijuana and on past Ensenada for a few miles. The other half was the final stretch into La Paz. In between were dirt

Fritz Kroyer plows through the Baja California brush in the 1972 Mexican 1000 in his Hi-Jumper single-seat VW-powered dune buggy. Kroyer, a two-time winner of the Mint 400 in Las Vegas, has never scored in Baja. This kind of terrain is especially tough to negotiate, and even harder on the car.

trails sometimes—in fact often—no wider than a single car and lined with brush and cactus. Not ideal for high speed driving, not even pleasant for the mules and horse carts that were the usual traffic.

Meanwhile in Newport Beach, California, a seaside community more famous for its bikinis, sandy shores, surfing and yachting, a sun-bronzed boat builder turned dune buggy enthusiast named Bruce Meyers was carefully studying the maps of Baja. He had a plan.

Meyers was plotting a course and at the same time, although he was unaware of it, charting history. In April 1967 Meyers and friend Ted Mangels took off from Tijuana in a Manx buggy headed south on a "feasibility" run. Instead of following the traditional route inland they found their way down along the west side of the peninsula from San Ignacio to Pozo Grande, bypassing Santa Rosaliá, Mulegé and the Comondús. They found the new route was not only much smoother than the Gulf trip, it was 30 miles shorter! When Meyers and Mangels reached La Paz they turned around and headed northward at full speed. They knew the course now, which eliminated much of the guess work necessary on the trip south, and made it back to Tijuana in only 34 hours 45 minutes. This was the first speed mark set by a four-wheel vehicle faster than that of any motorcycle. And it set the stage for an increasing amount of high-speed adventure south of the border.

Two months later, in June 1967, the first real race occurred in Baja California. It went off without fanfare, but again it was a major step toward the birth of off-road racing as it exists today. The race involved two Chevrolet V8-powered Toyota Land Cruisers, one driven by Claude Dozier and Ed Orr and the other by Ed Pearlman and Dick Cepek. The third and last vehicle in the race was a Meyers Manx handled by Drino Miller and journalist John Lawlor, ex officio historian of Baja racing.

The Ekins brothers and Mulder had made a multi-vehicle assault on the Tijuana-to-La Paz record. But they did it as a team effort, not in competition with one another. This new attempt would be an out-an-out race, with each vehicle driver doing his best to get there first. But, once again, the conquistadors would try a new course—the one devised for them by Howard Gulick, co-author of the *Lower California Guidebook* and a recognized authority on both the rugged peninsula and its primitive roads. The route took the racers east from Tijuana to Mexicali on a paved and winding highway, then south through San Felipe and Bahía San Luis Gonzaga where it joined the traditional route of Highway One north of Punta Prieta. Beyond Punta Prieta, however, Gulick's course left the main road again, heading down the west side of the peninsula through Miller's Landing and past Guerrero, but bypassing El Arco. From there it followed the beach route used by Meyers and Mangels on their pioneer run. The latest trip followed a 975-mile route, the longest Tijuana–La Paz run then or since. It also offered the most pavement—roughly 240 miles of asphalt, mostly on the Tijuana–Mexicali–San Felipe leg.

None of the three came close to touching the time set by Meyers and Mangels, but the Toyotas did establish a new mark for four-wheel-drive vehicles. Dozier and Orr drove the winning Toyota, completing the distance in 41 hours 45 minutes. Pearlman and Cepek's time in the other Toyota was 57 hours 12 minutes, while Miller and Lawlor made the trip in 67 hours 55 minutes. But the times, slow by today's standards, were not really what captured everyone's excitement. What really mattered was that three cars actually *raced* down the treacherous peninsula—and made it.

Fascination with conquering the awesome peninsula on wheels was beginning to build now, and the excitement even reached Detroit. Colorful tales of solo runs down Baja began appearing in motor magazines and added to the interest. But the idea of an organized event remained only a dream in the minds of a few. Someone, it seemed, was making a new attempt every few weeks now. In July 1967 two seasoned Baja adventurers, Spencer Murray and Ralph Poole, made one of the most spectacular and successful runs to date.

Employing their extensive knowledge of the peninsula, Murray and Poole worked out a route that used 240 miles of pavement from Tijuana to San Felipe and the beach route from San Ignacio to Pozo Grande. Across the central desert of the peninsula, however, it followed the main road through El Arco rather than the west coast road Gulick had recommended. The result was a total distance of 950 miles, the same as Highway One, but with the advantage of over 100 miles more pavement.

The new route proved to be a good one. Driving a Rambler American sedan, Murray and Poole sped from Tijuana to La Paz in a sizzling 31 hours flat. That shattered all previous records by all types of vehicles. The bikes, the buggies and the four-wheel-drive machines had all been beaten on their own ground by an ordinary passenger car. A second vehicle on the Rambler run, a Rebel SST hardtop with Jim Hanyen, Bob Thomas and Ken Piere aboard, didn't fare as well. Mechanical troubles forced it out of the run at Bahía San Luis Gonzaga after only 340 miles.

But this latest attempt, which American Motors intelligently capitalized on, had helped make the Baja run one of the most sought-after speed records in North America. An incident a short time later pointed out the need for some sort of organizational control. The idea was for one vehicle to leave Tijuana while another, almost identical car, was already heading down the peninsula on its way to La Paz. The trick didn't work.

Ed Pearlman and a small group of other off-road enthusiasts were already busy organizing NORRA and deciding which records they would recognize. The organization's first official act was to establish the 31-hour Rambler trip as the overall speed record from Tijuana to La Paz. Three earlier efforts also were acknowledged as records for certain types of vehicles. The 41-hour 45-minute trip made by Dozier and Orr was considered the official figure for four-wheel-drive machines, while Meyers and Mangels' 34 hours 45 minutes was set as the best time for dune buggies. The 39 hours 48 minutes it took the Ekins brothers and Mulder was established as the speed mark for motorcycles. At that time NORRA didn't separate two-wheel machines according to engine size, but Dave Ekins could claim that his original run in 1962 of 39 hours 48 minutes was a record for motorcycles of under 250cc displacement.

The National Four-Wheel-Drive Association had already verified the Dozier and Orr run, but that group had no interest in other types of vehicles. That meant that anyone seeking to set a record using a buggy, motorcycle or passenger car had to depend on Mexican police, tourist agencies and telegraph. Officials in Mexico had always been cooperative, but they had limited facilities and little or no way of keeping a close watch on the vehicles to make sure there was no cheating. But now that NORRA had established itself as a sanctioning body, there were definite targets to shoot for —and, of course, there were a number of eager speed enthusiasts waiting anxiously to try their skills.

The first assault on Baja under NORRA sanction was made by the late Bob Feuerhelm in September 1967. Feuerhelm fielded a team of five Jeeps in an effort to set a new four-wheel-drive figure and, hopefully, overall record as well. It was an elaborate operation by Baja standards in those days. Feuerhelm's budget was reportedly in excess of $25,000. For drivers he picked reigning Baja champs Murray and Poole, Baja veteran Cepek, the late N. C. "Speed" Boardman, Chuck Coye, Byron Farnsworth, Rod Fish, Bill Hardy, Lee Long and Ensenada police chief Tomás Villa Beltrán. The route was essentially the same as Murray and Poole had used in their record-setting run. Each vehicle was on its own in a race against the terrain and time, competing against each other the same way the two Toyotas and Manx buggy had a few months before.

Despite a generous budget and careful planning, the assault was aborted by Mother Nature. A few hours after Pearlman waved the Jeeps off in Tijuana, a hurricane hit the peninsula and brought the race to a hurried halt. It was one of the few races anywhere without a single finisher. In fact none of the contestants made it even half-way.

But if the first NORRA miniature event was something of a fail-ure, it by no means served as an omen of things to come. Baja California enthusiasts had been talking for some time about a full-scale race down the peninsula, involving considerably more than just a handful of vehicles. The idea sounded wild, but it stirred the imagination. Was it possible? Why not?

Pearlman and other NORRA officials began seriously discussing the possibility of such an event. Soon the excited chatter turned to serious planning. The first step was to approach the Mexican government. In a few months that lonely, forgotten peninsula would be headed for stardom.

1967 Mexican 1000

Pearlman found Mexican government officials enthusiastic about the proposed race. They viewed it as an opportunity to publicize Baja California and its tourist attractions. It also would be a dramatic demonstration that the roads to La Paz, however rugged and primitive, were passable in any type of vehicle that had been properly prepared. NORRA worked out a course that corresponded with the route Meyers and Mangels followed on their record run, but this time contestants would race from north to south.

In the interest of safety Mexican officials wouldn't allow the competing vehicles to run at top speed down the heavily traveled, 65-mile stretch from Tijuana to Ensenada. NORRA agreed to a false start in Tijuana, with a mandatory time of 90 minutes for the first 65 miles. The *real* start of the race would be in Ensenada.

Because the distance from Tijuana to La Paz was thought of as 1000 miles, the event would be called the Mexican 1000, even though its actual length fell short of that figure. The official course ran 915 miles from Tijuana and 850 miles from Ensenada. Between Ensenada and La Paz there would be five checkpoints where fuel would be available. The checkpoints were Camalú, Rancho Santa Ynez, El Arco, La Purísima and Villa Constitución. The route included about 70 miles of pavement south out of Ensenada and the final 100 miles into La Paz. The remaining 680 miles would be over narrow dirt trails.

On October 31, 1967, a field of 68 vehicles lined up just outside of Tijuana for the start of the first Mexican 1000. At midnight they started pulling out of the bordertown at the rate of one every two minutes. Once in Ensenada, drivers and crews climbed into sleeping bags to get a few hours of rest before the scheduled 6 A.M. start the next morning, when they would be flagged away at three-minute intervals.

Portrait of a man in a hurry. Above, Johnny Johnson heads for victory in the 1972 Mexican 1000, powersliding his single-seat Sandmaster around a dangerous curve near Camalú as excited spectators look on in amazement. Below, the winning style Johnson used in 1970 to win the big race. Despite such hard charging, Johnson is considered a steady driver with good finish record.

The next day Ray Harvick and Bill Stroppe, driving a Ford Bronco, set a blistering pace down the pavement and scored the fastest elapsed time into the first checkpoint at Camalú, 95 miles below Ensenada. But as the going got rougher, motorcycles began to take command. Larry Berquist, riding a Honda 350, cleared the second checkpoint, Rancho Santa Ynez, well ahead of the field and looked like a sure winner. But then the fateful electrical problems reported earlier knocked him out of the race while partner Gary Preston waited anxiously in El Arco for a teammate who would never arrive.

Now it was talented Malcolm Smith's turn to take the lead as he rode a Husqvarna 360 into El Arco, the halfway point, in 9 hours 45 minutes. This placed him well ahead of any four-wheeled vehicle. But luck wasn't with Smith and his partner J. N. Roberts, who took over at El Arco. Roberts, riding furiously fast, maintained the lead for several hundred miles. But riding along in darkness over unfamiliar terrain the young Californian lost his way—and with it, the lead.

Shortly after dawn the first vehicle arrived at the fifth and final check, Villa Constitución, 130 miles from the finish line in La Paz. It was a motorcycle, a Triumph TR-6 ridden by John Barnes,

Another sample of Johnson's style in the 1970 race.

who had relieved Dick Hansen at El Arco. But once again bad luck plagued a two-wheeler. When Barnes roared excitedly into town he couldn't find any checkpoint personnel to clock him through. As he rode up and down the main street of Villa Constitución, frantically and angrily searching for the officials, J. N. Roberts, who had finally found his way, arrived in town. Moments later a Manx buggy showed up with Vic Wilson and Ted Mangels inside. When Barnes saw them his enthusiasm died. The Manx had left Ensenada later than the motorcycle, so Wilson and Mangels were already well ahead of the bike in elapsed time.

The officials were finally located having breakfast in a local cafe, shocked and somewhat embarrassed. They hadn't expected anyone to show up that early. Time cards were promptly and properly certified and the three vehicles were off to La Paz.

The confusion and delay at the final checkpoint gave Wilson and Mangels just the slight advantage they needed to clinch victory in the first Mexican 1000. Most of the final miles of the race were on pavement where the buggy could reach a faster top speed than the motorcycles. So Wilson and Mangels arrived first in La Paz in a record 26 hours 8 minutes from Ensenada. With another 90 minutes tacked on to their time for the trip from Tijuana to Ensenada, they also earned a new Tijuana-to-La Paz mark of 27 hours 38 minutes.

J. N. Roberts, tired and somewhat disappointed, followed the buggy in, earning second place overall for Smith and himself with a time of 27 hours 18 minutes from Ensenada. Their figure from Tijuana, 28 hours 48 minutes, was a record for motorcycles, a full 11 hours under the 1966 mark posted by the Ekins brothers and Mulder.

Barnes and Hansen were third overall, 26 minutes behind Roberts and Smith. Despite the confusion at Villa Constitución, the close competition between cars and motorcycles was indicated by the arrival of another Meyers Manx, driven by George Haddock and Jimmy Smith, only 42 minutes behind Barnes for fourth place overall. In addition to overall victory, Wilson and Mangels had also captured top honors in the production two-wheel-drive buggy category, while Roberts and Smith had the fastest motorcycle over 250cc.

Other category winners and their times from Ensenada were:

Production two-wheel-drive passenger cars: Ak Miller and Ray Brock, Ford Ranchero, 32 hours 50 minutes.

Production two-wheel-drive utility vehicles: Orrin Nordin and Chuck Owen, Jeep DJ-6, 28 hours 35 minutes.

Modified and nonproduction two-wheel-drive vehicles: Andy "Pop" DeVercelly and Dick Archibald, Volkswagen buggy, 32 hours 48 minutes.

Production four-wheel-drive vehicles: Rodney Hall and Larry Minor, Jeep CJ-5, 29 hours 45 minutes.

Modified and nonproduction four-wheel-drive vehicles: Gene Hightower and Ed Vanable, Chevy V8-powered Jeep, 30 hours 32 minutes.

None of the motorcycles under 250cc completed the race.

1968 Mexican 1000

In the eyes of NORRA officials and most of those who competed in it, the first 1000 had been an unqualified success.

"I think the best thing about it, though," one official now recalls,

94

"is what we learned about racing in Baja and running a major event like this."

Several major changes were made for the second annual race. NORRA officials decided to eliminate the Tijuana-to-Ensenada leg entirely and start the race in the southern end of Ensenada. Three more checkpoints also were added, El Rosario, Punta Prieta and San Ignacio, bringing the total to eight. These forced some minor changes in the route which raised the overall distance a few miles. The increase in mileage, however, was offset by improvements to the road leaving Ensenada and heading into La Paz that brought the total amount of pavement to 220 miles.

Word spread quickly about the big race after the first event, and at six o'clock the morning of November 5, 1968, there were 243 vehicles, including motorcycles, in Ensenada for the start of the second Mexican 1000. This was nearly four times the number that had competed the year before. The starting interval was reduced to one minute, but with the increase in entries it still took more than four hours to flag them all off.

Spencer Murray and Ralph Poole, back at it with another Rambler, scored the fastest time into the first checkpoint, covering the 95 miles in a little over one hour. But no more than five minutes behind them were Parnelli Jones and Bill Stroppe in a Ford Bronco V8. At the 150-mile mark, well into the desert, Jones and Stroppe were ahead with a time of two hours. But just 17 minutes off their pace was a motorcycle, a Honda 350 ridden by Larry Berquist. This time the Honda's battery held up, and Berquist arrived in El Arco, the halfway point, leading the race with a time of 9 hours 30 minutes. This was 15 minutes under the figure set by Malcolm Smith over the same distance in the 1967 race. Gary Preston, glad to see his teammate this time, relieved Berquist on the Honda and took off in a hurry for La Paz. He maintained the lead at a rapid pace, but it was no runaway. Only 42 minutes behind was another two-wheeler, a Triumph TR-6 ridden from Ensenada by Don Bohannon and taken over at El Arco by Al Rogers.

The climax came as it had the year before at the final checkpoint, Villa Constitución. Officials were ready and waiting this time. And it was a good thing. Preston on the Honda and Rogers on the

Triumph cleared the final check, after more than 700 miles of rough racing through daylight and darkness, with exactly the same elapsed time!

But the two motorcycle aces didn't have the show all to themselves. Only 40 minutes behind, and with the fast pavement that favors four-wheel vehicles coming up, were Larry Minor and Jack Bayer in a Ford Bronco V8. It was going to be an all-out sprint to the finish with absolutely no margin for even the slightest error. At least that's the way it looked until the Triumph carrying Rogers developed engine trouble a few miles from the finish and Preston, riding flawlessly, roared into La Paz first as overall winner of the race with a phenomenal time of 20 hours 38 minutes—5 hours 30 minutes faster than Wilson and Mangels had made it the year before.

Rogers managed to nurse the ailing Triumph to La Paz to finish second overall 22 minutes behind Preston. Moments later Minor and Bayer arrived in the Bronco to win the four-wheel-drive category and take third overall with a time of 21 hours 11 minutes.

Other winners and their times were:

Production two-wheel-drive passenger cars: Ingvar Lindqvist and Ole Anderson, SAAB V4, 30 hours 29 minutes.

Production two-wheel-drive utility vehicles: Ak Miller and Ray Brock, Ford F-100, 25 hours 7 minutes.

Production two-wheel-drive buggies: Andy DeVercelly and Tom McClelland, Manx-type buggy, 22 hours 37 minutes.

Modified and nonproduction two-wheel-drive vehicles: Johnny Johnson and Paul Frank Schwab, Corvair buggy, 23 hours 44 minutes.

Modified and nonproduction four-wheel-drive vehicles: John Ulfeldt and Terry Weir, Buick-powered Mity Mite, 31 hours 43 minutes.

Motorcycles under 250cc: Whitey Martino and Steve Holliday, Husqvarna, 23 hours 17 minutes.

As those times indicate, competition in Baja off-road racing had grown considerably keener. A motorcycle had won overall, but only by a margin of 33 minutes over a four-wheel-drive machine. And in keeping with the trend, 13 vehicles bettered the mark set a year earlier by winners Vic Wilson and Ted Mangels. Six of them were motorcycles, four were buggies, two were four-wheel-drive rigs and one was a pickup truck.

1969 Mexican 1000

The third annual Mexican 1000 remained essentially unchanged from the preceding year. The same checkpoints and routing were used again, and a total 247 vehicles showed up for the start at 8 A.M. on October 30, 1969.

NORRA officials had decided to start the race a little later to avoid waking up too many Ensenada residents and to give everyone a little more sack time. The change was appreciated.

The first vehicle was flagged out of town under a sunny autumn sky while a crowd estimated at more than 5000 lined the main street of the seacoast port city to cheer on the contestants. Mexican military troops stood guard to prevent overzealous fans from crowding out into the road. Taco venders and ice cream peddlers pushed their carts along the roadside shouting invitations to gastronomic delight that were barely audible above the sounds of revving engines and the cheers of excited spectators. Young Mexican school girls and boys, dressed in their finest, scurried excitedly from one car to the next seeking autographs from every driver they could find.

Most of the four-wheel vehicles had not even left Ensenada when Ak Miller and Ray Brock, category winners in both previous races, scored the fastest time into the first checkpoint at Camalú. Driving a Ford pickup they covered the first 95 miles in 1 hour 6 minutes. But only one minute behind them were Ed Orr and Jon Woodner in a Datsun. Two minutes behind were regulars Spencer Murray and Ralph Poole in the Rambler. Also two minutes behind were two young Los Angeles area drivers, Steve Smith and Richard Smith, in a Ford Bronco V8. The Smiths, who were not related, sped out of Camalú and a few miles down the road collided with a buggy. The Bronco spun out of control, hit a dirt embankment and flipped several times. Despite the sturdy roll cage both of the young men, driving in their first race, were fatally injured.

As the race continued into the more rugged terrain, a motor-cycle moved into the lead. Malcolm Smith, riding a Husqvarna 250, was the quickest competitor to arrive at the midway checkpoint at El Arco, where partner Whitey Martino climbed on and headed south for La Paz. But Brock and Miller, the fastest team at the first checkpoint, managed to pick up the pace enough to grab the lead again by the time they made the final check at Villa Consti-tución. With good road ahead it looked like the Ford pickup had the overall win clinched. But a spindle broke a few miles out of the checkpoint and the two drivers waited more than seven hours for a replacement sent out to them from La Paz. As they waited alongside the road in the chilly darkness, a Bronco driven by Larry Minor and Rodney Hall raced by on the way to victory. Minor and Hall arrived in La Paz shortly after dawn with a time of 20 hours 48 minutes, just 10 minutes off the record set by Larry Berquist and Gary Preston the year before, but easily good enough for over-all victory and first place in the production four-wheel-drive divi-sion.

Finishing second overall and winning the nonproduction two-wheel-drive buggy class were Johnny Johnson and Dave Donnan in the homemade Corvair buggy. Third overall and second behind Johnson and Donnan, in what was then the same category, were Drino Miller and 1967 co-winner Vic Wilson in the revolutionary single-seat buggy Miller had designed. Wilson had driven the machine from Ensenada to El Arco where Miller took over for the final half of the race. Fourth overall and first in the production two-wheel-drive buggy category again were Andy DeVercelly and Tom McClelland with the Manx-style buggy. Fifth overall and first among motorcycles over 250cc were J. N. Roberts and Gunnar Nilsson with a Husqvarna 500. Their time was 21 hours 35 min-utes. Nilsson rode the last half of the race and made the best time for that stretch of anyone in the race—10 hours 29 minutes. Offi-cials were once again amazed at the keen competition. The first five vehicles arrived in La Paz within 47 minutes of each other. But more surprising was the fact that they represented four separate categories. Nothing so far had indicated what type of vehicle was tops in Baja.

Brock and Ak Miller finally made it to La Paz in their pickup with a time of 28 hours 4 minutes. It wasn't nearly as good a time as they promised before the spindle snapped, but it was still good enough to win the production two-wheel-drive utility vehicle category. Even with their lengthy delay out in the desert, they still beat the second place vehicle in their class by more than four hours!

Winners in the remaining categories were:

Production two-wheel-drive passenger cars: Ingvar Lindqvist and Sven Sundquist, SAAB V4, 25 hours 50 minutes.

Nonproduction four-wheel-drive vehicles: Bob Seivert and Dan Widner, Olds V8-powered Jeep, 23 hours 36 minutes.

Motorcycles under 250cc: Malcolm Smith and Whitey Martino, Husqvarna, 22 hours 25 minutes.

1970 Mexican 1000

By now the Mexican 1000 had established itself as a genuine classic motor race on a par with such celebrated international events as the Monte Carlo Rally and the East African Safari. Former Indianapolis 500 winner (1963) Parnelli Jones, frustrated by mechanical failures that sidelined him repeatedly, vowed to win the race—eventually. Many insiders figured this was the year he might succeed. Stroppe had decided to switch from the four-wheel-drive Bronco to a lighter two-wheel-drive version with a fiberglass body. The decision to switch paid off earlier in the year when Jones won the smaller Baja 500 in record time. Jones had frequently delivered stirring performances in major off-road races, but until the Baja 500 in June 1970, victory had always eluded him and Stroppe, who regularly went along for the ride, but left all the driving to Parnelli.

There was every indication that the race this year would again be faster than the preceding event. More drivers were experienced, cars were getting faster and more reliable and the course was expected to be faster also, by virtue of some major improvements. The president of Mexico was running for re-election and had made

Another hard charger who always thrills the fans is Mickey Thompson, seen here hurrying south in the 1972 Mexican 1000 with son Danny as co-driver. Despite brilliant and colorful driving style, Thompson has been plagued by mechanical woes in Baja.

a campaign swing down through the Baja peninsula a few months earlier. Preceding his trek was a bulldozer smoothing out the road. By November rains and wind had roughed up the route considerably, but it was still in good enough shape to promise faster racing in the interior wilderness.

Jones, feeling more confident since his Baja win earlier in the year, predicted the race would be won in under 18 hours—and that he and Stroppe would be first in La Paz.

"If it takes me longer than eighteen hours," Jones said, "I won't be able to drive it all myself—and that's the way I want to do it."

Jones also seemed more at ease with the new, lighter-weight two-wheel-drive Bronco. "Those four-wheel-drive rigs are okay," he said. "But you just can't get with it as well. They won't take it if you throw 'em around sideways all the time."

For the fourth annual Mexican 1000 NORRA revised its starting procedures. Previously, starting positions were assigned in the order in which entries were received. Before the date on which entries would be accepted for the 1969 race, one experienced team had a representative literally camped on the doorstep of the NORRA office in Glendale for one week. He was, naturally, first in line the minute the office opened, and claimed not just the first starting position, but the first 12. NORRA decided this kind of tactic was unfair to the private and amateur entrant who could not afford to spend a week standing in line to get a good starting position. So beginning in 1970 positions were determined by a drawing held a few weeks before the race.

Another change was made this year in classification of vehicles. The motorcycle category division was lowered from 250cc to 125cc, in hopes of attracting more small trail bikes to the event.

Pleasant sunny weather again greeted racers on the morning of November 4, 1970. Reports from farther down the peninsula hinted at a chance of rain along the route, but the showers never materialized. The first motorcycle started at eight o'clock sharp, and the first four-wheeled vehicle, a buggy, was given the green flag at 9 A.M. It was obvious after the race was underway for only an hour or so, and radio reports began arriving back in Ensenada, just how fast the pace was going to be. To no one's surprise, Jones and Stroppe were making the trip in record time. They cleared the third checkpoint, Rancho Santa Ynez, 240 miles south of Ensenada, in just 3 hours 33 minutes. Fans waiting around race headquarters in Ensenada for progress reports were stunned when an official posted Parnelli's time on the blackboard. Some cheered wildly, while others simply shook their heads in amazement and walked away.

In the excitement over Jones's fantastic performance, however, many missed noticing that Vic Wilson, driving the single-seat VW buggy, was only half an hour off the Bronco's pace when he cleared Rancho Santa Ynez.

But whether Wilson and his teammate Drino Miller would eventually have outdueled Jones and Stroppe will never be known. The Baja Jinx that had haunted Parnelli so long struck another blow. The Bronco snapped a rear axle before it even reached the halfway mark at El Arco. There seems little doubt, however, that Jones would have had to keep going flat out to score a win. Wilson reached El Arco from Ensenada in 8 hours 2 minutes, bettering the previous best motorcycle time to that point by 1 hour 28 minutes. When word of Wilson's performance reached Ensenada, whoops of joy filled the large hall at race headquarters where hundreds of fans and family waited sleepily for word on the high-speed adventure.

Miller jumped into the metallic blue buggy at El Arco and raced off to La Paz. At Villa Constitución, two motorcycles had cleared the final check before Miller arrived. They were a Yamaha 360 that had been ridden by Phil Bowers and Mike Patrick and a Husqvarna ridden by Whitey Martino and Malcolm Smith. Miller was only minutes behind in the single-seater, and because of his later starting position, was already ahead of them in elapsed time. But as the three charged down the final stretch of road, Miller passed both motorcycles to claim the honor of arriving first in town, in addition to overall victory in the race and in his class. He had taken 8 hours 5 minutes to drive from El Arco to La Paz. That, added to Wilson's record-setting time from Ensenada to El Arco, gave the team an overall figure of 16 hours 7 minutes. That shattered the record of 20 hours 38 minutes Larry Berquist and Gary Preston had set two years earlier. Wilson, an emotional man, was almost in tears with joy because he had become the first man to share an overall win twice in the 1000-miler. He had scored with Miller in 1970, just as he had with Ted Mangels in the first race in 1967.

Second overall and second in that same category was another single-seater that Chuck Andrade and Steve Rieman had shared driving chores in to finish the distance in 17 hours 24 minutes. Third overall and first in the production two-wheel-drive utility vehicle category was a Ford pickup driven by Walker Evans and Shelby Mongeon with a time of 17 hours 41 minutes. They beat the fourth overall and second in category Chevy pickup of Donnie Beyers and Doug Roe by a slim two minutes. Fifth overall and third in the category were perennial utility vehicle winners Ak Miller and Ray Brock. Their Ford pickup suffered eight flat tires, slowing them to a time of 18 hours.

Winners in other categories were:

Production two-wheel-drive passenger cars, Ingvar Lindqvist and John Ghini, SAAB V4, 19 hours 14 minutes.

Production two-wheel-drive buggies: Johnny Johnson and Larry Bright, Corvair-powered Bandido buggy, 18 hours 8 minutes.

Production four-wheel-drive vehicles: Sandy Cone and Gene Hightower, Jeep, 19 hours 2 minutes.

Modified and nonproduction four-wheel-drive vehicles: Bob Seivert and Dan Widner, Olds V8-powered Jeep, 21 hours 34 minutes.

Motorcycles under 125cc: Steve Hurd and Dub Smith, DKW, 21 hours 35 minutes.

Motorcycles over 125cc: Phil Bowers and Mike Patrick, Yamaha 360, 18 hours 31 minutes.

A total of 17 vehicles beat the previous Berquist and Preston record. They included one passenger car, three pickup trucks, four production buggies, four nonproduction two-wheel-drive vehicles, two production four-wheel-drives and three motorcycles over

125cc. It was a faster race, to be sure. But it was still remarkably evenly matched. Parnelli Jones, cheated once again from victory by mechanical failure, had become something of a folk hero in Baja. But he remained more interested in being a winner.

1971 Mexican 1000

Hordes of off-road racing fans poured across the border into Baja California in record numbers for the fifth annual Mexican 1000 and to join in the carnival-like atmosphere that had already become a legendary part of the event. But one subject seemed to dominate everyone's mind and conversation. Would this be the year fabled Rufus Parnell Jones finally broke the Baja Jinx?

NORRA had made some drastic revisions in its classification of vehicles for this year's race. With the decline of Manx-type buggies the production buggy category had lost its significance, and at the same time single-seat buggies like Drino Miller's were becoming increasingly popular. Consequently the production buggy and the nonproduction two-wheel-drive categories were eliminated in favor of the following:

Single-seat buggies and nonproduction or modified vehicles with only one occupant, and

Nonproduction or modified vehicles with two occupants.

In addition the production and nonproduction four-wheel-drives were combined into a single category. A new category also was created for the Baja Bugs, Volkswagen sedans shortened in both front and rear for off-road racing. And, for the first time, contestants were allowed to go the full distance solo. Previously those with single-seat cars or motorcycles were required to make a driver or rider change at El Arco.

There also was a minor route change this year. The main road on the east side of the peninsula was now paved through Santa Rosalía and Mulegé. It would be easy for a contestant to go from San Ignacio to Santa Rosalía and down through Mulegé, taking advantage of the high speeds the pavement would allow, and then cut back to the west side in time to make the check at La Purísima.

To prevent that from happening, NORRA established a new check-point at Rancho Cuarenta on the west side of Baja about halfway between San Ignacio and La Purísima.

Entries were down slightly for the 1971 race, only 222 vehicles including motorcycles took the green flag. The race began November 3, with the first motorcycle starting at 8 A.M. and the first four-wheeled vehicle waved off at 9 A.M.—the same as the preceding year.

Parnelli Jones and Bill Stroppe were in the same Ford Bronco Colt in which they had competed the year before, and very nearly dominated the race. The powerful V8 machine with its light fiber-glass body was placed in the new category for nonproduction or modified vehicles with two occupants.

From the time Jones, handling all the driving himself as always, pulled out of Ensenada it was his race, and his alone. Jones reached the first check at Camalú in one hour flat. He was through Rancho Santa Ynez in 3 hours 39 minutes, nearly an hour less than Vic Wilson had made it there a year earlier. Finally he and Stroppe reached La Paz, at long last, in a record 14 hours 59 minutes, a full hour and eight minutes faster than Wilson and Drino Miller had done it the year before. Both Jones and Stroppe were mobbed by excited *gringos* and Mexicans, and the hard-charging veteran racer mused later that fighting off the crowds was the roughest part of the race. But no one could have wiped that broad grin off his face for hours afterward.

Only one other driver had the slightest chance of catching Parnelli. That was Bobby Ferro, who ran solo in a single-seat buggy, finishing in 15 hours 16 minutes for second overall.

Jones and Stroppe also won the new category for nonproduction vehicles with two occupants, while Ferro won the class for single-seat buggies. They were the only two contestants in the race to better the previous year's record.

Winners in other categories were:

Production two-wheel-drive passenger cars: Howard Jenkins (solo), Volkswagen, 19 hours 47 minutes.

Production two-wheel-drive utility vehicles: Walker Evans and

Shelby Mongeon, Ford Pickup, 16 hours 21 minutes.

Four-wheel-drive vehicles: John Ulfeldt and Sandy Cone, AMX V8-powered Jeep, 19 hours 31 minutes.

Baja Bugs: John Steen and Mike Burke, 19 hours 59 minutes.

Motorcycles under 125cc: Terry Clark and Dean Goldsmith, Harley Baja 125, 21 hours 9 minutes.

Motorcycles over 125cc: Malcolm Smith and Gunnar Nilsson, Husqvarna 450, 16 hours 51 minutes.

1972 Mexican 1000

Both nature and NORRA officials made some major changes in the sixth annual Mexican 1000. A few weeks before the race a hurricane hit the peninsula washing out roads, uprooting trees and cactus, flooding towns and filling once powder-dry lakes and riverbeds with raging water. The association's changes were less dramatic, but no less significant to the participants. NORRA switched the start of the race northeast to Mexicali, bypassing much of the traditional route, including Ensenada. The new route headed south out of the Baja capital city on a stretch of paved road that had been ripped up badly by the flooding, to the first checkpoint at El Paraíso on the gulf coast. From there contestants headed inland across roughed-up mountainous roads where the heavy wind-whipped rains washed much of the soil away from rocks leaving a jagged, bumpy trail across the mountains. The route reached Camalú, where the remainder of the course was the same as preceding years. Originally NORRA had intended to send drivers and riders out of Mexicali on a route identical to the one Murray and Poole followed on their record run in 1967. But the hurricane made much of the east coast route impassable even for buggies and motorcycles.

"The course is about as bad as it was five years ago," said Doug Fortin after a hectic pre-run down the peninsula. "It's not a race track anymore."

While Parnelli made the trip to La Paz in 14 hours 59 minutes the year before, Fortin said he would not be surprised if the 1972 version required closer to 19 hours for the top finishers.

"Those guys who have machines built low to the ground, like Ferro's 13-inch wheels, may be in for some trouble," Fortin predicted. "Even the eighty-eight-mile stretch from Mexicali will be difficult. There are eight washouts along the pavement which means a lot of braking and one detour."

The storm had made many changes along the peninsula that Fortin said would make the going tougher than usual.

"Going along the road to El Rosario we saw a big bus and at least a dozen passenger cars stuck in the mud," he said. "In fact we buried one of our Jeep Wagoneers deep and it took us four hours to get it out."

Fortin predicted the course change and the effects of the storm would add considerably to the time it would take to run the race. "I'd say the new section of the course will add about two and a half hours and the nature of the roughness beyond will add another two and a half hours," he added.

"Before you went all out. Either you broke or you won." But this year it would prove to be a little trickier. In a section from Cuarenta to La Purísima, only 80 miles, Fortin and Clark took nearly eight hours.

"The bushes had grown about five feet tall and ours were the only set of tire tracks we could see," he said. "Apparently the rest have not pre-run that far."

But others had run the course in advance, and their observations were not much more encouraging than those of Fortin and Clark. The 1972 race promised to be perhaps the toughest and most challenging yet in the colorful history of off-roading in Baja California.

Before the start of the race many drivers and riders were still undecided which would be the best route to the coast—via San Vicente, 55 miles south of Ensenada to take advantage of the pavement, or through Mike's Sky Ranch high in the Sierra Mártir range which would bring them out just a few miles north of the second checkpoint at Camalú.

Bobby Ferro, runnerup in the previous 1000 and winner of the 1972 Baja 500, preferred San Vicente. "It's too dangerous around

Mike's Sky Ranch," he said. "Too many washouts, several places where you can't pass other cars because of the cliffs and ravines."

Ferro also was prepared for the unpleasant conditions along the way.

"I expect to hit a lot of mud, that's why I will have twenty sets of goggles along. But I expect to finish the race in about sixteen hours."

Johnny Johnson favored the Sky Ranch route.

"I figure there will be too much traffic the other way," he explained. "Besides, I feel most of the cars won't make it to Camalú."

Johnson, who got lost in the 1972 Baja 500 in June and was disqualified for missing a checkpoint, drew the 191st starting position, putting him far back in the pack.

"Maybe by the time I come through those ahead of me will have splashed out most of the mud and water off the trail," he said with a smile. "And I do my best driving at night because I concentrate on what I'm doing instead of trying to take in the scenery."

Concern over the new course and its rugged condition clouded much of the interest in a new class introduced this year by NORRA for the popular mini pickups being imported from Japan by Chevrolet, Ford, Datsun, Toyota and Mazda. Nevertheless the new class attracted a healthy number of entries, indicating that interest in running production vehicles was growing.

Parnelli Jones was heavily favored to win again this year, despite the popular view among drivers and riders that this might be the year of the pace rather than the race. But from the start, at 8 A.M. on October 31, five miles south of Mexicali, it was obvious that Jones wasn't going to let all those troublesome obstacles along the way slow him up even a little. Parnelli, with Stroppe along for the ride, covered the distance to the first checkpoint, La Purísima, in one hour—less than half the time most contestants predicted it would take.

The weather was nice when the race started, but a new contestant had entered the event—a storm that promised to make things nasty for anybody who didn't reach La Paz before it did. The new tropical storm was brewing up in the Pacific a few hundred miles south of Baja, and heading north rapidly. It broke up before reaching land, however, and contestants had nice weather the whole trip. The entire race was strictly Parnelli's show again. But there were moments . . .

Jones and Stroppe had blasted through every checkpoint leading the pack, and when they hit Villa Constitución it looked as if they had it made. They refueled and Stroppe gave the Bronco a quick once over, then they were off in a loud roar from the 351-cubic-inch engine and a squeal of the giant tires. But 15 miles from La Paz the Bronco sputtered to a stop. Jones, sick with disappointment, shook his head in dismay. Stroppe jumped from the Bronco and immediately began fiddling with the distributor points that had been giving them trouble since the start. But the Bronco refused to fire. Then Jones noticed the fluttering fuel pressure gauge.

"Out of gas," Parnelli told his boss. At their last stop at Villa Constitución a small amount of fuel had mistakenly been poured into a water jug instead of a fuel can carried on board. The jug was left behind, with probably just enough gas to carry them the remaining few miles. But there they sat, alone in the early morning darkness, certain victory ticking away by the seconds. As the two stomped and fumed in frustration, a pair of headlights appeared weaving slowly toward them. A VW sedan was making its way back from somewhere on its way to somewhere with several jovial occupants.

"Sí," they had plenty of fuel and even a siphon hose, but nothing in which to transfer the fuel from the VW to the Bronco. The VW's tank was lower than the race car's, so straight siphoning wouldn't work. Jones spotted a bottle of tequila that had been making the rounds from one sleepy reveler to another and after a financial arrangement had been agreed upon, the contents were poured onto the sandy road. It took 12 fifths of fuel to get the thirsty V8 rumbling again. The unscheduled pit stop had taken 45 minutes, but Jones and Stroppe crossed the finish line a few minutes later with an elapsed time of only 16 hours 47 minutes to win the race for the second straight year. They beat teammates Larry Minor and Jaime Martínez, who made it to La Paz in another modified Bronco in 17 hours 25 minutes.

Bobby Ferro's string of wins was broken. He flipped his black-and-gold-colored single-seater just before checkpoint four at Santa Ynez. Repairs were made, but the transmission packed up a few miles farther down the road and he never finished.

Johnny Johnson had better luck in the 1000-miler than he had earlier in the year in the 500. Johnson, who had replaced Ferro as driver for the factory Sandmaster team, completed the distance by himself in a single-seater to win his category in 20 hours 17 minutes.

Winners in other categories were:

Production two-wheel-drive passenger vehicles: Dick Lee and Rick Lee, 21 hours 53 minutes.

Production two-wheel-drive utility vehicles: Jimmy Jones and Cass Cassinelli, International Scout, 26 hours 21 minutes.

Four-wheel-drive vehicles: Bill Rush and Dan Shields, Bronco Colt, 20 hours 13 minutes.

Motorcycles under 125cc: Erick Jenson and Steve Hurd, DKW, 22 hours 8 minutes.

Motorcycles over 125cc: Gunnar Nilsson and Rolf Tibblin, Husqvarna, 19 hours 19 minutes.

Baja Bug vehicles: Ernst Schneidereit and Dieter Plambeck, 2180cc VW, 25 hours 14 minutes.

Mini pickups: Carl Jackson and Earl Morris, Courier, 24 hours 27 minutes.

Monaco. Indianapolis. Le Mans. All classics in their own realm. Races that have a certain excitement and magic. It's the same with the Mexican 1000—a single race that stands as the ultimate in off-road racing. But this wild high-speed odyssey in a charmingly primitive land has more to its credit than prestige. More than any other ingredient in a complex beginning, the peninsula challenge launched off-roading out of its status as a weekend hobby into the international arena of recognized sports, spawned a multi-million-dollar support industry and created fresh opportunities for scores of bored suburbanites.

6 READING THE ROAD

Andy DeVercelly leaned forward in a sort of confidential manner, stuffed a Kool Filter King between his lips and then paused before lighting it.

"I've known guys who got stuck in the dust—in a buggy. That's no bull," he said, and as he talked the unlighted cigarette wiggled up and down.

"And when they started to climb out of the car they tripped and fell and just sank into the stuff like you would quicksand. Just like . . . water . . . and you can drown in that stuff.

"I've never heard of anybody actually *drowning*. But I know a lot of guys who came damn close. I know it sounds ridiculous, but you have to see it to believe how it gets down there. I mean, if you fall down—you completely *sink*."

Andy paused to light the cigarette and then he went back to talking about—The Dust.

"I guess probably that's one of the worst things, because you can't escape it, you know. It's just *all* around you—all the time."

Andy stops to take a long thoughtful draw from the frosty glass of draft beer in front of him. All the talk about dust makes the cool brew seem especially soothing. Although Andy doesn't need any excuses. He is, he admits, a master beer drinker in classic *Oktoberfest* tradition. It doesn't show though. Andy DeVercelly, forty-two years old, is slim and solid. A transplanted New Yorker turned California buggista, DeVercelly is something of a guru among the growing band of mechanized masochists. He is master car builder, pioneer racer, consistent winner and even runs his own events out in the Anza-Borrego Desert northeast of San Diego.

"Just imagine," he says as he pulls in some of the mentholated smoke from the cigarette. "You ride along, bouncing, fighting the wheel, holding your breath as long as you can. Maybe a minute. Then, finally, you just . . . your chest is aching and burning and you need clean air, so you take a deep breath and . . ." He makes a grotesque face. ". . . all you get in your mouth is *dust*."

Baby-powder fine, gritty, suffocating dust. In the nose, drying, chafing the tender membranes. In the mouth, sticking like salted cotton to the tongue, soaking up every drop of saliva that might attempt to wash it away. Sifting into the lungs, and burning like hot ammonia fumes.

But the eyes are the worst. Drivers and riders, most of them at least, poke breathing holes in their goggles to let moisture out. But they inevitably let the dreaded, hated dust in.

"It's funny, though," Andy said. "This damned dust gets in your goggles and the moisture from your eyes—you know, the tears and normal perspiration from your skin—turns the dust to mud."

Really? Mud?

"Yeah, no foolin'. You'll be hauling down the road, slippin' and slidin' and these damned little weird mud balls are bouncing around inside your goggles just right in front of your eyes. It's just nutty as hell.

112

"So every few miles or so, you reach up—when you think you're gonna have time—and empty these damned little balls out."

There isn't much time. Every decision, every movement must be made within a fraction of a second. And it's those decisions that often make the difference between winners and those who wind up waiting in the desert beside a wrecked or broken buggy, motor-cycle, four-wheel-drive machine, Baja Bug or whatever.

Come into a blind corner, one that drops off to the left or right . . . into *nowhere*, a little too slow and disappointment floods your body. Precious seconds—lost. There are thousands of such curves in any off-road race. Take them too slow each time and those seconds quickly build into lost minutes, and maybe hours. But hitting them too fast can spell trouble for the unsuspecting or inexperienced chauffeur.

On the trail the hot desert wind rushes in over the short plexi-glass windshield and slaps us viciously in the face. The little yellow buggy rips along the narrow dirt trail, weaving around prickly cactuses and scratchy scrub brush that reaches out dangerously

Veteran racers advise keeping your foot on the throttle until you clear a jump like this or the buggy may nose over, a very unpleasant and undesired situation.

close. Andy's nasal voice is barely audible above the high-pitched whine of the Volkswagen engine just inches behind him and his nervous passenger.

"You just can't remember every corner," he yells, still keeping his dark brown eyes fixed on the treacherous road ahead, both hands gripping the small padded steering wheel.

"The bad ones you remember . . ."

A blind corner lies ahead. The dirt trail disappears quickly to the right around a clutch of bushes and cactus. The buggy is sailing along at nearly 70 mph. Andy reaches down with his right hand and shifts into third gear. The tachometer needle swings quickly up to . . . eight-thousand revs! A Volkswagen? You wonder when the valves are going to come flying out and splatter you in the back of the neck. The buggy's speed doesn't vary one mile per hour.

"You don't ever let off unless you're sure you have to," he explains. "But get into a lower gear and keep the revs up in case you have to—in a hurry.

"As soon as you get into the corner you've got to make a decision —quick. Two things . . ."

A wall of brush looms ahead, approaching at incredible speed, swallowing the road.

". . . is the curve too sharp to take at the present speed? If not, can you throw the car through sideways, in a powerslide? Or will you have to guide it through, following the ruts?

"If you're going to have to slow down, you need to do it with compression from the engine. That's why you downshift."

Andy charges into the blind corner, taps the brakes. There is no jerking movement, only the sudden thrust forward, the overwhelming sensation of reduced speed as the harness pulls you back against the seat. The car lurches sideways, but in a graceful gesture, and then is engulfed in a cloud of dust, a blanket of darkness. Hold your breath . . . wait for—something. The dust vanishes, bright sunlight returns and the buggy is headed off down the road in the right direction. Andy lets the engine rev tight before he drops it back to fourth gear. He will have a few seconds respite, maybe, before another such corner confronts him . . .

Back in the more serene and comforting environment of a cozy bar, Andy explains: "Concentration." A one word philosophy that is essential to survival. "You've got to learn to read the country, study how the rocks look and where they're located, be able to tell in advance which way the road goes.

"If the road is flat you may be able to slide around it, throw the car sideways. But if it's rutted and you try that you might end up on your head. That's why you downshift. You want to keep the engine speed up to either slow you down with compression or power on through. But you can't remember every corner or plan for them, and you're going to make mistakes once in a while."

Even when you make a bad decision you can still avoid trouble and save time if you know what to do.

"Say you're coming into a curve hard and fast. You dive into it and realize you're in too hot to maneuver it. What do you do?

"The usual reaction is to throw the car sideways or stand on the brakes—get the damned thing stopped. But that's the wrong thing to do. All wrong. The worst thing you can do, really. Just go straight ahead. Even if there are rocks and cactus ahead, chances are—nine times out of ten—you'll roll right on over them. But if you try to slide through . . . that's a good way to get upside down, or bust up the wheels and suspension."

Even Andy, a recognized master at reading terrain, doesn't always make the right move. He remembers many times when he has been overly cautious.

"I've hit corners too slow, not knowing what was around the bend, and then found a quarter mile straight ahead. I could have gone through all out, but . . . it's frustrating."

Even on closed courses, like Borego or Las Vegas, where participants make several laps over the same countryside in one race, it isn't easy to know how fast to keep the buggy moving.

"You may hit a ditch or a jump and know immediately you took it too slow. But the next time around there's always that element of fear that keeps you wondering if you should try it faster this time. And if so, how much faster? Five miles an hour? Ten? Eleven? You just don't know for sure until you're over. And if you've misjudged, there's no second chance . . . at least not that time around."

And, of course, in Baja there's no second chance—period. Not, at least, until next year. Then things will probably be entirely different. The weather likes to play games with the land. Games that keep racers guessing inch by inch.

"You can pre-run a course one day and it will be a helluva lot different the next. The course even changes a lot during a race. If it's muddy to begin with it may dry up as the race goes along—or it might get muddier. Or it might be dry in some spots and muddy in others. You have to be alert to all these conditions."

Concentrate on the present and plan for the future, all at the same time. It's a mind boggler. Unlike road or circle track racing where drivers and riders know exactly when to let off on the gas, hit the brakes, shift and accelerate, off-roading doesn't offer this luxury. It's a continuous guessing game, a battle with the odds, hoping to get the advantage . . . at least part of the time. And how are the other guys doing? Did Ferro or Parnelli muff that corner too? Will Johnny Johnson get crossed up and waste valuable time? You try to force those thoughts out of your mind. There isn't room for them. Take care of business at hand. Concentrate. Keep this thing rolling.

"Most guys have trouble pacing themselves," Andy explained. "That's one of the toughest things to learn. You wonder if you're going fast enough—or maybe too fast and tearing hell out of the car."

For Johnny Johnson it's always a fight to keep from slowing down and daydreaming.

"I enjoy riding along," Johnson said. "And all of a sudden I realize I should speed up, that I'm not really driving as fast as I should be. I have to keep pushing myself."

For others it's just the reverse.

"I need a co-driver to keep me under control," said Mickey Thompson. "Or else I sometimes get carried away. I'll go as hard as I can. I've never crashed, but that's still not good. It's hard on the equipment. You have to pace yourself, not go any harder than necessary. It's tough to find a happy medium."

Parnelli agrees. "It's tiring," he said, "because you never have time to relax. At Indianapolis and on most road courses there are usually places where you can sit back for a few seconds and kind of let your shoulders and arms, and nerves, relax and unwind. But not in Mexico or at Vegas. You're fighting the car and the road all the time. It's exhausting—mentally more than physically."

Most off-roaders prefer running with a co-driver, particularly in the long races like the Mexican 1000.

"As I always say," Andy grinned, "it's nice to have someone along to share the frights."

A co-driver can make a big difference psychologically. Someone to talk with, even if you have to yell a lot. Companionship on a long and lonely odyssey. It's comforting. Keeps the spirits up.

"Your co-driver can make a big difference in your attitude," Andy said. "He can help relieve the tension. Les Choat is one of my favorites for that. He's a helluva good driver himself, and if you make a mistake he'll kid you about it. Not in a nasty way, but, you know, make you laugh. And he likes you to do the same. It's more important than you can imagine."

Johnny Johnson, who won the single-seat buggy class in the 1972 Mexican 1000, hates to ride alone.

"I'll talk to myself when I'm alone," he said. "Anything to know you're still alive. It's pretty dreary.

"If you've got a co-driver along and you go bounding down the road, lose it for a second and get all crossed up—maybe spin around and bounce off the road—then save it, he'll nudge you with his elbow and say something like, 'Nice save, guy,' and laugh like hell. Those things break the tension and keep you looser and more alert, in better spirits."

Remain cool, Andy insists. Keep control of your mind, body and the machine. Lose control of any one and you soon blow the ballgame. It's like dominoes. If one falls, they all follow. Talk to yourself too. Out loud. It keeps you more aware of what's going on and what you're doing. Like mental therapy. Sort of a safety valve to let off steam. Cussing is good too. It relieves frustration quicker than anything, even a cold beer. And don't worry about that knot in your stomach. That's just fear. It's supposed to be there. As Parnelli himself said a few years back, "If you ain't scared once in a while—you ain't goin' fast enough!"

"You've got that fright with you all the time," Andy said. "Wondering what's around the next corner. Is somebody broken down . . . maybe blocking the road. Or maybe somebody just poking along . . ."

Those things happen in off-road racing. There aren't any course workers around to wave flags warning of slower traffic or unsafe conditions. It's all up to the drivers. Take your chances. You won't know what's on the other side of that curve till you get there, partner. Sure, it's scary.

"Anybody who says he isn't scared out there is either a liar or a fool," Andy said. He took a swallow of cold tap beer and lit another cigarette.

"I get scared a thousand times during a race. You come up on a corner and the first thing you realize is that you're going too damned fast. You try this and try that, every damned thing you know, and you get through. Somehow you manage to get through and you feel . . . sort of . . . excited all over. Pleased with yourself. Then you start asking, 'How in the hell did I do that?' "

But you don't have much time to worry about it. More action is coming at you—fast as hell. ". . . always turning right or left it seems," Andy was saying. "You have to pay attention—con-cen-trate," he says, sort of stretching out the syllables to make the point stick. "The guy who doesn't concentrate is the one who winds up running off the road . . ." He demonstrates with a gesture of his hand.

Many drivers, Andy among them, see advantages to night driving over daylight.

"You don't have to worry as much about coming over the hill or around a corner and clobbering someone," Andy said, "because you can usually see their light. In that respect it's easier to drive at night."

118

On a motorcycle the consequences of making a minor mistake in off-road racing can be painful. Bike riders used to dominate the sport, but improved skill and equipment now gives four-wheel vehicle drivers the edge in most races.

But there are problems that come with darkness. Dangerous ones.

"It's a lot easier to get lost in the dark. You can't see a thing much except for a few feet in front of you. And that's scary too, and dangerous, because you're driving beyond your lights. If you see something ahead you may not have time to stop unless you're chugging along slow."

Arriving at a checkpoint usually offers a brief respite for drivers and riders in off-road enduros. But just as in road and circle track racing, the pit stop can decide a lot about where a team will end up at the finish.

"I've had my most frustrating problems at checkpoints," said Johnny Johnson. "I'd explain to my co-driver what had to be done while we were stopped, and they'd forget something.

"I guess in all the excitement and confusion they just forgot, but it sure is aggravating."

Most of the top teams work out some sort of system before they hit the road, even rehearsing several times before the race so they can perform like a well-disciplined drill team.

Andy described how he works it:

"As we approach a checkpoint, whoever is riding as co-driver will take the time card and hand it to the official when we pull up. Both of us get out of our harnesses before we even stop. After stopping we both climb out, and the guy who had been driving checks the car—fuel, oil, tires—anything like that. He also gives the suspension the once over to make sure nothing is about to break. If it is, better stop right there and fix it. Same is true out on the road. If you notice any strange sounds, stop and check to see what it is and fix it then if possible. You might lose time stopping, but avoid having an accident later or really tearing something up if you kept going.

"Anyway while the guy who has been driving is checking the car, the new driver climbs in and buckles up. Then the new co-driver jumps in, grabs the time card (don't forget that, whatever you do!) and we take off. Then the co-driver can fasten his lap belt and harness before you pick up much speed and get into the rough stuff."

Andy is convinced that a good co-driver must also be a competent driver, even if he never takes a turn at the wheel himself, and a good mechanic. Bill Stroppe never relieves Parnelli during a race, but he is an accomplished off-road racer—and no one in the world knows more about fixing a Bronco.

"A good co-driver can help you read the terrain and make quick decisions. He'll also know if you're going too fast or too slow (never a problem with Parnelli, of course). He can also help you remember the route, maybe even remember bad places you don't.

"As a rule when I pre-run a course I try to remember all the bad places, spots where I might get into trouble. I don't worry about the smooth spots. You should always take the co-driver along on the pre-run, and both of you talk about it as you drive along. It isn't necessary to go very fast, just get a feel for the road."

Some teams take notes along the way, sort of a running diary, even if they don't use them in the actual race. This seems to help them remember certain spots long after they've passed them. It doesn't hurt to type the notes and put them in something like a small notebook that can be referred to easily. That way the co-driver can serve as something of a real navigator and keep the man at the wheel posted on what is ahead.

"We've always worked out some kind of signals, too," Andy explained, "to alert the driver of danger, a bad spot in the road, a pothole, ditch, washout, bad curve, anything like that."

Knowing how fast, or slow, to drive still remains one of the biggest stumbling blocks to success in off-road racing. It's never easy, even for the seasoned veterans.

"That's something that takes a long, long time to learn," Andy said. "Some guys pick it up quicker than others, it just depends on instincts I guess."

It's the same old bugaboo about when to use the gas and when to use the brakes. As the legendary Dan Gurney once put it: "A race car has a gas pedal and a brake pedal, and a race driver is supposed to have a brain to tell him when to use which one."

But there are circumstances unique to off-road racing that require special expertise. Like knowing what to do if you're sailing down the road in a buggy at about 90 mph and suddenly come upon a series of deep potholes along the crumbling asphalt pavement. That sort of thing happens a lot in Baja, and there's only one way to handle it.

"You keep your foot in it all the way," said Andy. "If you were to travel over that road at 10 miles per hour it would jar you and the buggy to pieces. But at seventy or faster you fly right over them, you never know they're there.

"There's a stretch of road in Baja where there are potholes two and three feet wide, and just as deep. They're along a fairly straight stretch, so you can drive fast. One year I was flying along over them, it was a smooth ride and Tom [McClelland] was perfectly relaxed. He didn't even notice how deep they were. But then for

Sometimes the course is pretty confining, but not hard to follow. Here a buggy zigzags through a dry wash, a common phenomenon of desert racing. Sudden rainstorms can fill these washes with raging water three feet deep, and more, in minutes, making navigation a little tougher.

some reason he looked out the side and saw how big they were, and from then on every time we'd go over one he'd flinch a little."

Hitting those bumps can be touchy business.

"Every thing has to be done just right," Andy said. "Even the slightest variation in speed can send a buggy rolling end-over-end. Like if you hit the crest of a hill or some kind of jump, the car has to be at the right angle when you land or over you'll go. Even if you don't flip, you'll get all crossed up and lose time trying to get straightened out again.

"The speed isn't always as important as how you handle it. Keep your foot on the gas until you're airborne, then let off quick or you rev the engine too high. But you must stay on the gas until the rear wheels clear the hump or the car will nose over on you. Then as soon as it sets down again, get on the gas. But smoothly. And be sure while you're in the air the wheels are straight."

Andy advises not to go flying off jumps like that if you have to turn immediately afterward. That sort of thing will always cause trouble. But if you do get the hang of it, don't worry about hard landings. Andy swears that if the job is done right you will hardly know when you hit the ground. "You should barely feel it," he promised.

But sometimes that can depend on what's down there when you arrive back on earth. In the Baja 500 there is a long stretch of fairly straight road approaching Gonzaga Bay with a series of rolling hills and dips. Since many cars and motorcycles are hitting top speed along there, they fly off each knoll and soar 10 feet or more above the ground and sail 30 or 40 feet through the air before hitting the ground again.

"One year Tom and I were just flying off of those one after another," Andy said. "I had a good rhythm going. But then as we went flying off one hill we looked down and right where we were going to land was a big rock, right in the middle of the road.

"You have to set a buggy up right before you go airborne, but once in the air there isn't a damn thing you can do to change direction. We just sat there and waited for the crash. "But luckily we just clipped the rock with a rear tire and kept going. It punctured the tire, but it held out until we made it to Gonzaga."

There have been times when Andy didn't get off to such a good start. One year in the Mexican 1000 he said he was racing across Lake Chapala, a sea of dust except after a major storm or hurricane, at about 95 mph when he hit a ditch and went sailing off into space.

"Everything would have been fine," he said, "except that it surprised me. I couldn't see because of the dust, and before I could do anything I was in the air sailing along 10 feet off the ground at 90 mph. I hit the ditch at a slight angle and when the car came down it landed sideways.

"I had a helluva time getting it straightened out, but I finally saved it [and went on to win his class]. Fortunately there wasn't anything around to hit. If there had been rocks and brush I'd have been in trouble."

Sometimes it's hard to remain cool and keep your mind on driving and eyes on the road. There are some things you shouldn't look at while racing—they sort of destroy courage, turn otherwise daring racers into cautious slowpokes. All it takes is one glance over the edge of a mountain trail. Those deep canyons are breathtakingly beautiful, but they do nothing for the competitive spirit. In many places in Baja the race follows narrow trails up and down steep mountains where a buggy or motorcycle could plunge several hundred feet into brush-and cactus-lined canyons.

"And those roads down there don't have any guard rails either," Andy laughed. "So always keep your eyes on the road. You can't let them spook you. Start looking down . . . you aren't gonna make it. Chances are you'll pull over and stop."

It's really no problem, Andy said reassuringly, as long as you can read the road correctly. "By reading the road right you can always tell which way the car will slide. You have to do that before you get into the corner."

Yes. Good idea, Andy. No argument there. And one important word of warning comes from several top buggy jockeys, stay off the brakes as much as possible.

"Never hit a hole with the brakes locked up," Andy said. "Always let the wheels roll free. If you don't, you'll get a flat tire almost every time. The rim will cut right through the tire or tube. Use the gears for braking as much as possible. You can't win a race with brakes, but then you can't win without them, either."

Bobby Ferro will attest to that. In the 1972 Mexican 1000 Ferro was among the front runners until the brakes failed in his single-seat buggy. His pit crew in Camalú tried to make adjustments, but halfway through the race Bobby entered a corner too hard, couldn't stop and rolled the car. He survived the shunt unhurt and nursed the buggy to the next checkpoint, but the spill had damaged the transmission enough to knock him out of the running a few miles farther down the road.

"Every inexperienced driver has a tendency to use the brakes a lot in off-road racing," Andy said. "Because the terrain demands so many changes in speed. But you have to force yourself to rely more on gears."

As described earlier in this chapter, Andy suggests downshifting when approaching a curve, keeping the engine revs up and not slowing down. Then, depending on the situation, the driver can either power on through the corner or let off on the throttle and let the engine slow the buggy. The popular heel-and-toe method (working the brake with the ball of the foot, while the heel is used for the accelerator) isn't practical in off-road racing. For one thing the Volkswagen clutch-brake-accelerator assembly isn't suitable for it, the accelerator pedal is too low. Trying it would almost require a double-jointed ankle—a rather uncommon phenomenon. Power is another factor. Parnelli Jones has the horsepower under the hood of the Bronco to motor through corners in grand dirt track fashion—using the throttle as much as the steering wheel for control. But the VW and Corvair engines, like most small powerplants,

Mickey Thompson doesn't know what's waiting for him on top of this hill, but off-road racers learn to read the terrain and pace themselves accordingly. Sometimes, of course, even the best get fooled, but that's all part of the game.

just don't produce that kind of power even at high revs. The Bronco also has an automatic transmission, which frees P.J. to use his left foot for braking, while the right foot is working the gas, or he can heel-and-toe if he chooses.

"You can hear Parnelli coming down the road, winding through the corners, rum-a-rum-a-rum-a . . ." said one old buggy pit crewman. "It's an exciting sound, sort of gives me chills to hear it. Reminds me of the old days when he drove midgets and sprints."

Powerslides may be the quickest way through corners in a two-wheel-drive machine, but trying the same technique in a four-wheel-drive vehicle, as Parnelli found out, won't always bring about the desired results. With power to all four wheels it's necessary to motor more or less straight through corners. Getting into a slide can slow you down, and trying to get out of it can be tricky.

"You can't throw a four-wheel-drive around," Parnelli said. "That's the trouble we had with the first Bronco. If you dive into a corner and try to bring the back around and then stand on the gas, you may find yourself going the wrong direction."

Some desert hazards can't be avoided. Like cactus. The terror of even the most fearless off-road racer, sharp cactus needles often seem to jump out at you like a frightened cat, clawing their way through thick driving suits and jackets deep into tender flesh. Not many desert veterans have escaped this painful ordeal.

"I slid off the road once just a little," Johnny Johnson remembers, "and brushed one of those big chollas [pronounced choy-yus]—damn!—did it hurt. I had cactus stuck in my arm, neck and shoulder. By the time I got to the next checkpoint my whole side ached and I could barely use my arm."

He had to spend valuable time pulling the two-inch-long needles out before getting under way again.

But even staying on the road is no guarantee of safety. Andy DeVercelly was hit in the chest with a chunk of cactus flipped up at him by the front tire while he was driving. "I was lucky it didn't get me in the face," he said. "But it hurt the most when I tried to pull it out. I was driving along steering with one hand and trying to pull it out with the other. It wouldn't come loose, and when I'd pull it felt like my chest was coming out with it."

But of all the hazards that confront off-roaders as they plunge through the wilderness, most agree their fellow racers are the most unpredictable.

"You know those rocks aren't going to move," Andy said. "But when you come up behind another car you never know for sure what the driver is going to do. For one thing he may not see you because of all the dust. That's where a good co-driver is important. While you're busy driving, looking at the road, he can keep a lookout for anyone approaching from the rear. You won't believe this, but sometimes—and this is especially true in places like Las Vegas —I've been right alongside another car and didn't know it. Only a few feet away and couldn't see it. It gets that dusty out there!"

But even when visibility is good it takes more than nerve and skill to pass another vehicle.

"The other driver may move over and you think he did it to let you pass, but actually he may have been just dodging a rock or something in the road. "If you start around him without any warning, he might plow right into you. You don't assume anything."

And once the novice off-road racer finally gets the hang of things, he soon finds out the fun is just beginning.

7 . . . AND THEN SOME OTHER STUFF HAPPENED

—————————————————————————→

If it had not been for rain, fog, a light that wouldn't work, three broken chains, two cows, a horse and a truck traveling the wrong way, DeWayne and Gary Jones might have won the Baja 500 in 1971. But success in off-road racing is always a little chancy.

The two Jones brothers, both in their early twenties, shared riding chores this particular year on a 250cc Yamaha prepared and entered by their father, Don Jones of Hacienda Heights, California. Considering the obstacles they were up against, neither of the lanky youths complained about finishing only third in category for motorcycles over 125cc displacement.

The bad luck began bombarding them shortly after leaving Ensenada a few minutes past noon. It started out as a nice enough day . . .

"DeWayne broke a chain a few miles south of town," Gary said. "He got off and fixed it, which took only a couple of seconds really, and took off again. It wouldn't have been so bad if it had only happened once, but the damned thing broke on him three times before he reached San Luis Gonzaga (the halfway point)."

DeWayne had other problems too.

"I was storming down the road flat out," he recalls, "When all of a sudden through the dust and blur I saw a truck up ahead. At first I thought it was in the race and I was catching it. "Then I realized it was coming at me from the other direction."

What happened in the next couple of seconds isn't too clear to DeWayne. It was one of those hazy sort of experiences that seem to combine slow motion and stop action, filled with a lot of mixed bits and pieces of emotion. He said he laid the bike down even though he was hitting around 100 miles per hour. Fear, anger and disgust all charged through his confused mind in one quick wave of sensation. The grinding sound of metal clashing with asphalt. The bouncing. Waiting. Anticipation of . . . what? Then the truck was on top of him. But no pain. Everything stopped. Quiet. No move-ment. For a brief moment DeWayne waited. Waited for something else to happen. Then his mind snapped back to the reason he was out there in the first place. Racing.

"He was really lucky," Gary said. "The truck belonged to a local resident. DeWayne didn't get hurt and the only damage to the bike was bent handlebars. "When he arrived in Gonzaga I straight-ened the handlebars while DeWayne fixed the chain. Then we gassed up and I took off for San Felipe."

Those little shunts along the way can slow a body down.

"If he hadn't had all that trouble," the boy's father, Don, said, "DeWayne would have been the first bike into Gonzaga."

But the team made some of their own mistakes too.

"We were waiting with gasoline a few miles north of the first checkpoint to refuel DeWayne," Don said. "When he came by he was lying down over the handlebars and really flying. He passed four bikes just as he went by and didn't see us. "We jumped into the truck and started after him because I knew darned well he wouldn't last more than another mile if he didn't refuel. But he must have realized it was us jumping up and down beside the road and waving, because about the time we all got in the truck he came over the hilltop on his way back."

Gary said he rode the final half of the race because DeWayne is the better road racer of the two and "I'm better at night." (Much of the first half of the Baja 500 is on pavement, and the majority of the true off-road portion is run after dark.) Gary said his half of the race was one near mishap after another, and that heavy fog and rain hampered his progress every foot of the way.

"It was just wet enough to be kinda muddy. I had to take my goggles off, finally, because I couldn't see through them. The dirt was better than the pavement though. When I hit the pavement at Ojos Negros, twenty-six miles from the finish, it was really slippery. I almost went down a couple of times, but I managed not to."

Gary said he narrowly missed hitting a couple of cows and a horse, but managed to keep the motorcycle under control.

"I saw a lot of eyes looking at me along the roadway," he said. "You know how animals' eyes glow at night when the lights hit them. That was prettty spooky."

But Gary said he almost didn't have any light.

"I rode as long as I could without turning them on. Then when I did, they wouldn't work."

It turned out that a wire had vibrated loose on the rough ride. But Gary found the trouble and fixed it within a matter of minutes.

Literally thousands of such colorful stories are carried out of Baja each year by the men and women who live them. How much is fact, and how much is fiction, doesn't really matter. The fact is off-road racing anywhere can be tough on the ego, and the bigger the ego the more it hurts.

"If I had any sense I'd just quit," said a tired and dirty James Garner after his Oldsmobile Cutlass broke down and left him stranded for seven hours in the cold and lonely wilderness of Baja California at night. It happened during the 1970 Baja 500, and Garner won't soon forget those miserable hours he spent out there . . . wondering, waiting.

Fritz Kroyer of Santa Susana, California, backs up his single-seat Volks-wagen-powered dune buggy after overshooting finish line in Mint 400. Kroyer, a Danish-born Californian, had just won his second straight race in Las Vegas, the world's richest off-road event. Kroyer was hampered by the blinding dust and required a relief driver, but had to take over the wheel again after only one lap when his substitute turned ill.

"While I was standing around out there trying to keep from freezing and going crazy, I kept asking myself what the hell I was *doing* there. But . . . I'll be back. I don't know why."

Off-road races are notorious for frustrating movie and speedway stars and creating their own brand of celebrities. Such as the two young San Diegans who tackled the Baja 500 in a homemade buggy the same year Garner had his troubles. They had serious doubts about even finishing, but they did more than just finish. They won their class and parlayed an $800 investment (cost of building the buggy) into a $3000 profit. Doug Fortin and Dick Clark, newcomers to the sport then, finished the race in 14 hours 27 minutes. But there were moments, they said, when it all looked pretty grim. About 14 hours 27 minutes worth of moments, to be exact.

"Things started out bad right from the first and seemed to get worse as we went along," said Fortin.

The team was the last to leave Ensenada. They pulled out of the small seaport city in their Corvair-powered buggy at about 5 P.M. with only about two-and-a-half hours of daylight driving ahead of them. But that was only the start of their woes.

"We were only twenty miles out of town when the engine seized up on us," Clark said. "Apparently we got a little anxious to get rolling and we were driving it too hard. We stopped and let it cool off for about fifteen minutes, added a couple of quarts of oil and took off again."

Fortin and Clark had never been in a Baja race before, and they were competing in a tough class that included Chuck Coye in a Baja Boot, one of the four-wheel-drive, V8-powered buggies built at General Motors by engineer Vic Hickey. Bud Ekins and Guy Jones were overall winners of the race the year before in one of these powerful four-wheel-drive buggies.

"We didn't think we had a chance against the Boot," Clark said. "For one thing, it has much more power."

And the darkness . . .

"Driving at night you can't see more than a few feet in some places," Clark continued. "You'll be clipping along at eighty miles an hour or so, and suddenly there's a great big rock in the middle of the road."

Taking wrong turns is easy, too, the drivers said.

"Sometimes it's hard to tell where the road is supposed to go," Fortin said. "You really have to be alert and careful."

One motorcyclist from Los Angeles, who managed to complete the 558-mile race, said he nearly had to walk the final 200 miles back to Ensenada. The rider said he fell on a lonely stretch of road while traveling at about 80 mph and was knocked unconscious. When he regained his senses it was so dark he couldn't find his motorcycle. Then when he finally did find it, he took off in the wrong direction and traveled several miles before meeting another competitor and getting straightened out.

Buggy drivers find the trail tricky too.

"We were hauling cookies down the road at about ninety-five," said Bob Thomas of Los Angeles, who was co-driver of a buggy one year, "when all of a sudden there just wasn't any more road."

Thomas said they hit a washed-out spot a few miles north of El Rosario and their buggy went airborne, landed on its nose, then careened into a ditch.

"I couldn't see a thing for all the dust," Thomas said. "When it finally cleared we saw that a wheel had been ripped off."

That was the end of the race for Thomas and his partner Bob Sinclair. They said five other dune buggies also fell prey to that same rut before the race was over. One of them, Thomas said, flipped end over end with both driver and passenger walking away unhurt, but very disgusted.

"That sort of thing is easy to understand when you've been out there at night," Fortin said. "You can't see much of anything, and what you see all looks the same."

Fortin and Clark said things went fairly well for them on that first outing—until San Felipe, a sleepy fishing village on the gulf coast of Baja California. That was when the rear-wheel-drive broke.

"We finished the rest of the race with just the front-wheel-drive operating," Fortin said. "That gave us some handling problems, especially in the sand. And we were afraid we'd ruin the front tires."

Fortin and Clark, who since have scored a number of victories in off-road events from Baja to Las Vegas, also found out later that the Corvair engine had received a "Baja bore job" on its maiden voyage. That's when the engine's air filtering system fails and the dust enters the internal parts of the powerplant and scratches the cylinder walls.

"It was really a mess," Fortin said. "We lost the air cleaner early in the race, and it [the engine] was really scarred up."

Sometimes the dust works on humans in the same fashion. One year in the Mint 400 Fritz Kroyer was forced to seek first aid and driver relief while leading the race because of painful eye irritation caused by the powdery menace. Trembling with pain after the silt had worked its way under his goggles and scratched his eyeballs, Kroyer described the ordeal:

"It was like you were driving in a darkroom. Every time you bumped into something, you had to fall back and go around it."

But even without the dust there is more than enough agony. Bob Thomas, writing in the Los Angeles *Times* about his first adventure in the Mexican 1000 in 1968, vividly described the frustration that so often follows off-road racers:

"As we were poised for the start at dawn Tuesday, the starter broke the tension with a signal. Gentlemen, set your watches back sixty years.

"And that's the kind of 'race' course it was—dirt, rock, sand and knee-deep silt, reminiscent of road conditions during the turn of the century . . ."

Thomas and his co-driver Mike Jones were plagued with misfortune from the start. As Thomas put it: "Our car, the Bugetta, left the starting line at Ensenada at 6:12 A.M. Our first problem didn't occur until 6:13 A.M.—at one hundred miles an hour."

They didn't know it then, but the steering arm which connects to the right front wheel was broken in half. Only one bolt was holding the wheel in place. It sheared several hours later—fortunately when the buggy was creeping along at about 10 mph.

Less than two hours into the race things started happening—too fast. The accelerator stuck at half throttle. "We nursed the car into the second checkpoint, El Rosario, one hundred fifty-two miles from the start," Thomas said. "There our crew, which had driven ahead the night before, made quick repairs with a helping hand from Mickey Thompson, the Bonneville racer.

"Then we headed into the roughest sections of the run, and the throttle stuck again—wide open. The only way to keep going was drive with one hand and switch the ignition key on and off with the other, using the engine in brief spurts. It was exhausting to fight the ruts, rocks and chuck holes that way, and after an hour and a half we stopped to trace the problem. We had progressed only 25 miles from the second checkpoint."

Forty-five minutes later the duo had located the trouble, sticky throttle linkage, and returned to the race. But a few minutes later a front spring mount broke. It somehow wedged into the chassis and at least held the assembly in place, but lowered the road height to six inches. Not enough for fast running.

At 5 p.m. Thomas and Jones pulled into Rancho Santa Ynez. They had covered 86 miles in eight hours, stopping twice to fix the steering arms and twice to coax the engine back into operation. The slow driving and dust had fouled the spark plugs and the engine died on them repeatedly.

When they arrived in Santa Ynez, Thomas said the place looked like a wrecking yard with twenty-seven cars under repair. Parnelli had been through earlier in the day, setting a record pace. But the big Bronco was tiring from the battering and hard driving, its wheels wobbling and the engine blowing oil. "We'll drive it till it falls," Parnelli said as he and Stroppe roared out of town. It did. Ten miles down the road.

Part of the crew for Thomas and Jones had flown ahead to Santa Ynez. As soon as the buggy arrived they started to work rebuilding it, welding the steering arm, replacing the lights that wouldn't work and jacking up the springs for more clearance. Four hours later the team was back on the road. They stayed in motion only twenty minutes before the engine stalled again. Three clean plugs brought it to life once more. Off again over bumps, down through rough dry washes and across the dark and lonely desert.

This strange sight greeted spectators at the finish line of the Mint 400 one year when the crippled dune buggy limped into the pits with its co-driver leaning out one side to take weight off the broken wheel and keep the buggy going.

Shortly after midnight the engine quit again, this time on a cold mountaintop. In the company of cows and a full moon, Thomas and Mike Jones changed the points, condenser, rotor, plugs and coil, and then pressed on toward Punta Prieta, the next checkpoint 76 miles away. They arrived there at 5 A.M. to huddle around a warm fire and refuel. Their average speed? A terrifying 9 mph.

They headed out of Punta Prieta, and as the buggy inched its way through a cactus-lined canyon, the right rear shock absorber mount broke. They were finished. It was the end of the race. They were out in the middle of God-knows-where, hungry, tired, cold, with a four-mile walk ahead of them to reach the nearest village, where they sat eating chocolate chip cookies and waiting for help to arrive. And the buggy? It was hauled out of Baja a few days later on the back of a truck, a twisted and patched testimony to what happens in off-road racing when things don't go well.

But it can be a rough road even for the successful. When Bobby Ferro, the rugged Hollywood stuntman with a sort of Sal Mineo kind of gentleness about him, won the Baja 500 in 1971, he pulled to a stop, kissed his future wife, Marlene, and said: "My legs are shaking. Give me something to drink."

Ferro had just spent 11 hours 11 minutes at the wheel of a single-seater dune buggy to become the first man to win a race without benefit of co-driver or navigator. During that time on the road, Ferro didn't make any relief stops. When his lovely fiancée remarked that he was all wet, Ferro just smiled and replied: "Of course, honey, I didn't have time to stop for *that*!" And he wasn't kidding.

Asked about other problems, Ferro said: "Some of the slower guys wouldn't move over. I had a lot of trouble just getting by other competitors. "I almost crashed twice dodging cows, I had to swerve to avoid them and got all crossed up. But once I got on the pavement [the last twenty-six miles from Ojos Negros to Ensenada], I said, 'Thank God.' I knew then it was all downhill."

There are always some chilling brushes with disaster, too.

"I was tooling along pretty good when it happened and my shoulder harness saved me," one off-roader explained from his hospital bed in San Diego after a bone-breaking crash in the Baja

500. Joe Francis said he was negotiating curves through the coastal mountains north of San Vicente at about 75 mph in his single-seat buggy when the left rear wheel flew off.

"I have been in all of the Baja races out of Ensenada," he said, "and have yet to finish one of them. But usually it was the machine that broke down."

Francis said he was only about 40 miles out of Ensenada when the stud bolts holding the wheel, apparently weakened in a previous race, sheared off and sent the wheel flying.

"The buggy nosed up on an embankment," he said. "It was a very sudden stop. My helmet flew off, but my shoulder harness saved me."

Francis praised the Mexicans for the quick medical attention he received. He said a nearby resident came to his rescue and took him to the first-aid station at San Vicente where he was treated before friends loaded him in the back of a camper and transported him to San Diego some 100 miles away.

"Those Mexican doctors did a great job," Francis said. "I'm sure glad as hell they were around."

Nearly everyone who tackles Baja has his or her share of wild tales to tell later. More than one weary off-roader has reported seeing strange sights along the way as they become physically and mentally exhausted. The world turns into a frightening animated cartoon. Giant cacti wave like prehistoric creatures. Lakes suddenly appear, blocking the way, then vanish quickly back into the foggy depths of a tired mind, where they were born. Nerves, strung tight from hours of tension, short-circuit reflexes. Mental signals sent to the hands and feet are lost en route. Concentration becomes a monumental task. The whole show, engulfed in aching exhaustion, is performed in slow motion. Minutes last for agonizing hours. Muscles resist orders. Mutiny. Put down the rebellion. Concentrate. Stopping wouldn't help. Turning back will only delay the relief. And add disappointment and shame to all the other misery.

"You wonder why you started," said one racer. "And then you remember. There really is a place you're going. You keep telling yourself that. Over and over. And you just set your goals a few yards at a time . . . the next bush, rock or curve . . ."

Sometimes the inner struggles interfere with the right decision, a decision that must be made in a tenth of a second. Then in another tenth of a second you know something went wrong, but . . .

Lynn Wilson, a thirty-six-year-old Canoga Park housewife and mother of four boys, riding a 125cc motorcycle, made a wrong turn and . . . crunch! She bounced off a boulder, damaged the bike and dislocated a finger. Darkness. Quiet. Loneliness. The head-lamp on the small two-wheeler was broken. It was hours before dawn. Impossible to continue in the darkness. Lynn built a fire and waited. She talked to herself. Brooded. Hoped.

"It was dumb . . . a bad mistake," she said later in disgust. "It seemed a long, long time out there in the desert . . . in the middle of the night, waiting for sunup. "There were coyotes and *bandidos* running around. Boy, was it scary."

Lynn had taken over the motorcycle from her eldest son, Bob, in El Arco. Bob had been more than two hours late in arriving because of a broken wire connecting the headlamp. Her nerves were already jittery before she climbed on the motorcycle around midnight. And then the painful crash. As soon as it was light enough, Lynn made her way south, arriving in La Paz at 9:37 A.M. with a time for the team of 34 hours 1 minute.

But it wasn't the crash or the injured finger that bothered Lynn Wilson the most. "That last stretch of pavement from Villa Consti-tución to La Paz was . . . so boring," she complained. "I wish the whole race was on dirt."

Lynn is no novice at this business. She is seasoned at taking all the lumps and bruises synonymous with desert riding. Nearly every weekend she and the family head for the desert to compete in races. She often puts in 100 to 150 miles each weekend in two-wheel enduros.

"Afterward I often just get on my bike and ride some more for the fun of it, maybe another hundred miles," she said. "I just love to ride my motorcycle, that's all it is. I keep in real good shape and don't get tired. As far as getting tired is concerned, a lot of it is all in your head."

The dislocated finger Lynn suffered in Baja wasn't her first injury or the worst. In two previous crashes while racing, she has busted a collarbone and a leg. "You just expect that," she said. But she won't go near the street. "It's too dangerous on the freeway. And the street is really dangerous. I won't ride on either. And besides, it's no fun on the pavement."

Family teams are increasingly frequent in off-road events everywhere. Terry Hildebrand, who operates a nursery in Vista, California, a rural community north of San Diego, took his eldest daughter Debbie, sixteen, on the Mexican 1000 in 1972, and it was "pretty neat . . . an experience," the teenager said. They drove a 1600cc Datsun pickup to fifth in their category after making the 912-mile run from Mexicali to La Paz in 35 hours 40 seconds. Hildebrand, a former motorcycle racer, said he is raising "a family of racing girls." And he has four to work with.

Both Hildebrand and his daughter agreed the final 120-odd miles of pavement were the roughest, and most boring. After more than 32 hours on some of the world's worst non-roads, "I was hallucinating," Hildebrand said. "I couldn't focus my eyes. I thought there were potholes where there were none." His percep-

Single-wheel landings like this are common in rough terrain, but they aren't recommended as the best way of doing things. Preserving the vehicle is as important as making good time. This kind of antic is tough on equipment and passengers.

tion was faulty, too. Dangerously so.

"I didn't think we were going fast, even though we were hitting speeds up to a hundred miles an hour. The cactuses were waving. We couldn't even tell which way the signs pointed."

Why suffer such an ordeal? Pure masochism? Not at all, Hildebrand insists. "In this race we were closer as a team, as people, as a father and daughter, than I would have thought possible. "I really don't know how to say it . . . we really had to, and did, understand each other. It was a terrific, outa-sight experience for me."

Not all the drama is confined to what happens on the road. There was Mickey Thompson, one of the super leadfoots of motor racing, a legendary speed king, beckoning to the dozens of spectators who had gathered around his lame Chevrolet pickup.

"Who will help me, please?" he almost cried. "I will give anyone a hundred dollars for a drive shaft. One hundred dollars—right now."

Out of the crowd stepped Jim Jenks, a bushy-faced man from Solana Beach.

"You can have the drive shaft from my Ford," he told Thompson, pointing to a shiny, new wagon parked on the side of the pits at Camalú, the second checkpoint in the Mexicali-to-La Paz version of the Mexican 1000 in 1972.

Thompson, reputedly a millionaire, dug into the pocket of his coveralls and pulled out a thick wad of bills—tens and twenties. But Jenks refused the money, saying it was worth it just to help a racer like Mickey Thompson continue, and perhaps finish, one of the toughest contests in sports. Thompson's drive shaft looked like a twisted pretzel, having been knocked into a useless state by a large rock on one of the bouncy dirt sections.

This is what the outsiders, and even many newcomers, don't understand. When everything is clicking, you run hard, as hard as you can. Make the other guy work to catch you, or to keep you from catching him. But if a guy breaks . . . well, that takes all the fun out of it.

"So much racing is cutthroat," said Andy DeVercelly. "Winning is everything. But in off-road racing, *participating* is the main thing

Making repairs along the way is always unnerving and frustrating, but something off-road racers must be skilled at to survive. Here Danny Thompson, Mickey's son, chomps on an apple while he and dad perform emergency field repairs at checkpoint Camalú in 1972 Mexican 1000. Danny regularly serves as co-driver to his father and helps build race cars.

. . . winning is only a fringe benefit."

Jenks had come to the Camalú checkpoint only as a spectator. He ended up a saviour. "I race cycles and I dig the racers," he said. "We all stick together when we're in trouble. It's a brotherhood."

But how was he going to get back himself? It is more than 150 miles from Camalú to the border, and another 40 miles from there to his home.

"At first I didn't think about it," Jenks said. "It was an impulse thing. Help the guy. I know how he feels. Then I got to thinking, so I asked Thompson if there was a way he could get me back home."

But Thompson and his heavy-duty pit crew were too busy ripping the drive shaft out of Jenks's truck to answer. An hour later Thompson was out of the woods and motoring happily on the route, barely remembering the name of a face in the crowd who stepped out to lend an unusual hand.

You can watch the start, you can watch the finish of a Mexican 1000, but there's no way you can get the real flavor of what off-roading is all about without visiting a pit stop like Camalú or El

Arco. Each November, as the Mexican 1000 contestants roar through the dusty little hamlets, local residents turn the event into a holiday. Kids cut school. The elders forget about harvesting corn, milking cows or plowing the fields. This is bigger than New Year's, Independence Day and Christmas combined. Crazy *gringos* flying, bouncing and sliding their vehicles over roads, through washes and brush-covered gullies and along dirt trails carved from years of horse traffic. The Mexicans watch—sometimes silently, other times laughing, waving, singing, cheering, applauding. Sometimes throwing rocks.

One year Thompson and his co-driver, drag racing star Danny Ongais, had barely gotten on the road when a Mexican youth tossed a rock through the windshield of the truck, splattering glass into the eyes of Ongais. "Danny wanted to continue," Thompson said. "But when I looked over and saw the blood all over his face, we turned around and headed back to Ensenada." Thompson said he saw a group of people, both adults and children, standing alongside the road waving and jumping up and down. Then—wham! "I don't know who threw it," Thompson said. "It made me mad as hell, but you can't stop to fight over something like that when you're racing. Besides, the kid probably never thought about what effect a little rock would have when it hit a truck head on at more than a hundred miles an hour."

Ongais received medical attention back in Ensenada, as did Thompson, who also had a glass splinter in one eye. Both recovered without permanent injury.

But most spectators gather along the course to watch in amazement at what can often turn into a spectacular horror show—without their help. Just outside of Camalú a group of about two hundred locals staked out a viewing spot on a dusty hillside to watch the action on a twisting section of the road that winds its way in sinuous S-curves down the hill and across a brush-covered valley. Most drivers and motorcyclists eased their way along, knowing the potential dangers waiting for the overzealous. Some, like Thompson, Parnelli, Andy DeVercelly and Johnny Johnson, seemed to hit it just right, swinging their vehicles through, using up every inch of the road in graceful powerslides. But others . . .

At day's end, seven four-wheel vehicles and five cycles had tumbled down a 30-foot embankment at almost the same spot in the road, crunching the landscape with a ku-boomp, whump, clank. Dust and silence. Although no serious injuries were reported, several out-of-control vehicles barely missed the spectators.

"This is the worst piece of the course," said Bob Hayes, a member of a pit crew not far from the dangerous curvy section. He spent a good part of the day flagging down racers, warning them of the road ahead.

"But most of them don't pay attention," he said. "They just barrel into the turn, hit those moon crater ruts and—boom—they go flying off the road. Just luck nobody was killed."

Hayes reaffirmed the belief of many of the participants.

"This has to be the roughest I've ever seen. Half the cycles are lost somewhere out there. The whole thing is horrendous. I would say fifty percent of the cars are either lost, busted or something in between. We don't know where they are."

Barbara Weed, a practical nurse, sat in the Camalú pit station and shook her head sorrowfully. "This race is becoming a freaky speed test," she said. "The cars are going a hundred and forty miles an hour in stretches and the road is not up to it. Someone is going to get killed if this keeps up."

Barbara has been involved in five of these races, mostly as a member of the medical team which patches the injured.

"We had one death [actually two] in the race three years ago," said Barbara. "Now the race is so competitive. The big car companies, Ford and General Motors, are getting in it under the table. The emphasis is on speed and winning, not fun anymore."

Most of the nine checkpoints from Mexicali to La Paz are equipped with doctors for emergency use.

"Camalú has a good doctor; he's a war vet and he knows what he's doing," Barbara said. "But some of the checkpoints have butchers. So we have to watch out and go in there ourselves when there is a need."

It is high noon at Camalú, a small agricultural community of roughly 1000 inhabitants. Today, however, there are several thousand more in town. Pit action is fierce as guys like Bobby Ferro roar in. Most have a problem of one sort or another.

"No brakes," shouts Ferro, who five months earlier won the Baja 500. "I can't stop this thing."

But nothing can stop Ferro either. At this point he is only 12 minutes behind Parnelli Jones, the early leader. To hell with brakes.

Another buggy driver, Mike Rose, pulls into the pits looking like a creature from the black lagoon. Bugs are splattered all over his teeth and nose and goggles. He can't see and he can't breathe.

"Ran into a whole section of nothing but bugs," said Rose. "Couldn't see where I was going."

A helpful soul takes a wash rag and wipes Rose clean. A full gas tank, a quart of oil, a Pepsi and he's back on the road.

Another driver barrels into the pits running on three wheels. He lost the entire front section on the Valle Trinidad portion, a 127-mile stretch from the east to west coast of Baja.

There is a nasty side to all this speed and thrills. Twisted minds have their own special sick ideas about humor—or something. At the S-curve, which proved to be quite a dropping off point, some spectators urge drivers to head toward the danger area, waving arms and laughing as they take their turn at the twisting, bumpy section. Some drivers luckily ignore the instruction. Others fall into the trap, sliding off the cliff and almost tipping over.

Back in the pits a "helpful" lad tells one of the drivers that there is a "bad section of road up ahead. A hairy curve. Big ruts. Take it at seventy because if you slow down, you will have to almost stop to get through it."

The driver nods approvingly and heads toward the horrible S.

"There's a lot of this kind of stuff going on," says Dick Lilly, sometime driver of off-road races. "You have to be good to see through the trickery. You have to know what is happening. I'm not running in the race this year but I'm itching to get in next year."

What's the attraction?

"I guess it's the fact the whole thing is really suicidal," said Lilly. "Isn't that far out?"

144

INDEX

145

National Off-Road Racing Association (NORRA), 14, 16–17, 23, 25, 36, 42, 47, 62, 71, 88–90, 94–95, 97, 104–106, 108
Nilsson, Gunnar, 98, 106, 110
Nordin, Orrin, 94
Núñez, Rodolfo, 23

Ohrdorf, Gottfried, 59–62
Oldsmobiles
  engines, 99, 103
  see also Banshees; Cutlasses
Ongais, Danny, 142
Orr, Ed, 75, 86–89, 97
Owen, Chuck, 94

Patrick, Mike, 56–58, 102–103
Pearlman, Ed, 14, 86–90
Penny, J. R., 18–19
Piere, Ken, 88
Pismo Beach races, 14, 17
Plambeck, Dieter, 60–62, 110
Plimpton, George, 54
Plymouths, 43
Poole, Ralph, 87, 95, 97, 106
Porsche brake assemblies, 59
Preston, Gary, 57–58, 92, 95–96, 98, 103

Ramblers, 95, 97
  American, 88
Rancheros (Ford), 94
Rebel SSTs, 88
Rieman, Steve, 55, 103
Riverside Grand Prix, viii, 6, 10, 16, 50
Riverside International Raceway, 16
Roberts, J. N., 56, 92–94, 98
Roe, Doug, 103
Rogers, Al, 95–96
Rose, Mike, 144
Rush, Bill, 110

Saabs, 96, 99, 103
Saginaw power steering, 9
Sahara-Nevada Corporation, 37
Sandmasters, 44, 50, 52, 110
Schneidereit, Ernst, 59–62, 110
Schwab, Paul Frank, 54, 96
Seivert, Bob, 99, 103
Shields, Dan, 110
Sigwardt, Peter, 7
Sinclair, Bob, 133
Small, Tom, 38–39, 41
Smith, Dub, 103
Smith, Jimmy, 94
Smith, Judy, 44

Smith, Malcolm, 57, 92, 94–95, 98–99, 103, 106
Smith, Richard, 97
Smith, Steve, 97
Smith, Val, 44
Snore 250, 50
Society of Automotive Engineers, 7
Springer, Bonnie, 12
Springer, Fred, 11
Springer, Pete, 11–12
Steen, John, 106
STP Novis, 43
Stroppe, Bill, 7, 11, 32, 46–47, 83, 92, 95, 99–102, 105, 108–109, 120, 135
Sundquist, Sven, 99
Switzer, Max, 56

Tacoma wheels, 61
Thomas, Bob, 88, 132–136
Thompson, Danny, 49, 57
Thompson, Mickey, 34, 38, 47–49, 57, 116, 134, 140–142
Tibblin, Rolf, 110
Toyotas, 43, 87, 89
  Land Cruisers, 56, 86
  mini pickups, 108
Trevor, Ted, 75
Triumphs, 83, 92, 95–96

Ulfeldt, John, 96, 106

Vanable, Ed, 94
Villa Beltrán, Tomás, see Beltrán, Tomás
Volkswagens, xi, 7, 9, 12, 44, 47, 50, 55, 59, 62–73, 75, 79, 81, 94, 102, 104–105, 109–110, 114
  clutch-brake-accelerator assemblies, 125
  engines, 1, 7, 21, 52, 61, 64, 125–126
  steering dampers, 60
  see also Baja Bugs; Sandmasters

Wampuskitty VWs, 50
Weed, Barbara, 143
Weir, Terry, 96
Westward Ho 200, 1971, 50
Widner, Dan, 99, 103
Wilson, Bob, 138
Wilson, Lynn, 138–139
Wilson, Vic, 55–56, 93, 96–98, 102–103, 105
Wolff Motors, 59–60, 81
Woodner, Jon, 97

Yamahas, 57–58, 102–103, 128
Younghusband, Ken, 56